GOD'S WORD
FOR A JR. HIGH WORLD

Friends

Gospel Light

Junior Church
Aug. 2003

Carla LaFayette, Author
Kara Eckmann Powell, General Editor

Gospel Light is an evangelical Christian publisher dedicated to serving the local church. We believe God's vision for Gospel Light is to provide church leaders with biblical, user-friendly materials that will help them evangelize, disciple and minister to children, youth and families.

We hope this Gospel Light resource will help you discover biblical truth for your own life and help you minister to youth. God bless you in your work.

For a free catalog of resources from Gospel Light please contact your Christian supplier or contact us at 1-800-4-GOSPEL.

PUBLISHING STAFF

William T. Greig, Publisher

Dr. Elmer L. Towns, Senior Consulting Publisher

Dr. Gary S. Greig, Senior Consulting Editor

Jill Honodel, Managing Editor

Pam Weston, Editor

Patti Pennington Virtue, Assistant Editor

Christi Goeser, Editorial Assistant

Kyle Duncan, Associate Publisher

Bayard Taylor, M.Div., Senior Editor, Theological and Biblical Issues

Kevin Parks, Cover Designer

Debi Thayer, Designer

Aimee Denzel, Illustrator

Natalie Chenault, Contributing Writer

You may make copies of portions of this book with a clean conscience if:

- you (or someone in your organization) are the original purchaser;
- you are using the copies you make for a noncommercial purpose (such as teaching or promoting your ministry) within your church or organization;
- you follow the instructions provided in this book.

However, it is ILLEGAL for you to make copies if:

- you are using the material to promote, advertise or sell a product or service other than for ministry fund-raising;
- you are using the material in or on a product for sale;
- you or your organization are **not** the original purchaser of this book.

By following these guidelines you help us keep our products affordable.

Thank you,

Gospel Light

PRAISE FOR PULSE

There is a cry from this generation for truth. **Pulse** curriculum targets this cry by leading teenagers to the Truth. How exciting it is to have a curriculum that gives the depth through Scripture and fun through involvement. —**Helen Musick**, Youth Specialties National Resource Team member, national speaker and author

The **Pulse** curriculum is truly "cross-cultural." Built on the solid foundation of an understanding of junior highers' unique developmental needs and rapidly changing culture, it affords teachers and youth workers the opportunity to communicate God's unchanging Word to kids growing up in a world that increasingly muffles and muddles the truth. —**Walt Mueller**, President, Center for Parent/Youth Understanding and author of *Understanding Today's Youth Culture*

The creators and writers of this curriculum know and love young teens, and that's what sets good junior high curriculum apart from the mediocre stuff! —**Mark Oestreicher**, Vice President of Ministry Resources, Youth Specialties

Great biblical material, creative interaction and USER FRIENDLY! What more could you ask? This stuff will help you see your junior highers reach their potential as disciples of Christ! I highly recommend it! —**Ken Davis**, President, Dynamic Communications International and award-winning author and speaker

It's about time that curriculum produced for junior highers took them and their youth workers seriously. **Pulse** does it and does it very well! This curriculum knows Junior Highers and proves that teens changed by Christ who are equipped and empowered by His Church really can change their world! I am planning to recommend **Pulse** enthusiastically to all my youth worker friends. —**Rich Van Pelt**, Strategic Relationships Director, Compassion International, author, speaker and veteran youth worker

I found **Pulse** to be a stimulating, engaging and spiritually challenging curriculum for middle school students. Kara Powell has developed a rich resource that provides teachers with strong content to teach and creative options to help teachers meet the individual needs of their students. Recognizing that spiritual formation is not an end in itself, **Pulse** provides a strategy for evangelism in each lesson that empowers students to share the gospel with their peers. This is a curriculum that makes genuine connections with middle school students and the culture in which they must live out their faith every day. —**Mark W. Cannister, Ed.D.**, Chair, Department of Youth Ministries, Gordon College

Written by veteran junior high youth workers who know how to communicate so kids will get the message! Kara has given youth workers a fresh tool that's user-friendly and geared to make a lasting impact by addressing the foundational issues of Christianity that sometimes take a back seat to trendy topical studies. —**Paul Fleischmann**, Executive Director, National Network of Youth Ministries

This is serious curriculum for junior highers! Not only does it take the great themes of the Christian faith seriously, but it takes junior highers seriously, as well. Young adolescents have a tremendous capacity for learning about spiritual things and this curriculum makes it possible for them to learn all they can about the God of the Bible— who loves them and wants to involve them *now* in His church. This is the best I've seen yet. —**Wayne Rice**, author and Junior High Ministry Director, Understanding Your Teenager seminars

Friends

CONTENTS CONTENTS CONTENTS CONTENTS CONTENTS

Unit I: Friendship Builders *Oct, 03 – Dec. 03*

Unit II: Friendship Wreckers

....You've Made the Right Choice in Choosing Pulse for Your Junior Highers

The Top Ten Reasons...

10. Junior highers equate who God is with what church is like. To them a boring youth ministry means a boring God.

Fun and variety are the twin threads that weave their way through this curriculum's every page.

9. Junior highers need and deserve youth workers who are expert trainers and teachers of biblical truth.

Every book is pulsating with youth leader tips and a full-length youth worker article designed to infuse YOU with more passion and skill for your ministry to junior highers.

8. Junior highers need ongoing reminders of the big idea of each session.

Wouldn't it be great if you could give your students devotionals every week to reinforce the learning goals of the session? Get this: YOU CAN because THIS CURRICULUM DOES.

7. Some of our world's most effective evangelists are junior highers.

Every session, and we mean EVERY session, concludes with an evangelism option that ties "the big idea" of the session to the big need to share Christ with others.

6. Since no two junior highers (or their leaders) look, think or act alike, no two junior high ministries look, think or act alike.

Each step comes with three options that you can cut and paste to create a session that works best for YOUR students and YOUR personality.

5. Junior highers' growing minds are ready for more than just fun and games with a little Scripture thrown in.

Scripture is the very skeleton of each session, giving it its shape, its form and its very life.

4. Junior highers learn best when they can see, taste, feel and experience the session.

This curriculum involves students in every step through active learning and games to prove to students that following Christ is the greatest adventure ever.

3. Tragically, most junior highers are under challenged in their walks with Christ.

We've packed the final step of each session with three options that serve to move students a few steps forward in their walks with Christ.

2. Junior highers tend to understand the Bible in bits and pieces and miss the big picture of all that God has done for them.

This curriculum follows a strategic three-year plan that walks junior highers through the Bible, stopping at the most important points along the way.

1. Junior highers are moving through all sorts of changes—from getting a new body to getting a new locker.

We've designed a curriculum that revolves around one simple vision: Moving God's Word into a junior high world.

Moving Through Pulse

Since **Pulse** is vibrating with so many different learning activities, this guide will help you pick and choose the best possible options for *your* students.

THE SESSIONS

The six sessions are split into two stand-alone units, so you can choose to teach either three or six sessions at a time. Each session is geared to be 45 to 90 minutes long and is comprised of the following four steps.

IT'S YOUR MOVE

A training article for you, the youth worker, to show you *why* and *how* to see students' worlds changed by Christ to change the world.

This first step helps students focus in on the theme of the lesson in a fun and engaging way through three options:

 MOVE IT—An active learning experience that may or may not involve all of your students.

 CHAT ROOM—Provocative, clear and simple questions to get your students thinking and chatting.

 FUN AND GAMES—Zany, creative and competitive games that may or may not involve all of your students.

The second step enables students to look up to God by relating the very words of Scripture to the session topic through three options:

 MOVE IT—An active learning experience that may or may not involve all of your students.

 CHAT ROOM—Provocative, clear and simple questions to get your students chatting about the Scripture lesson.

 PULSE POINTS—A message outline with simple points and meaningful illustrations to give students some massive truths about Scripture with hardly any preparation on your part.

STEP 3
MOVING ON

This step asks students to look inward and discover how God's Word connects with their own worlds through three options:

CHAT ROOM—Provocative, clear and simple questions to get your students chatting.

REAL LIFE—A case study about someone (usually a junior higher) who needs your students' help figuring out what to do.

TOUGH QUESTIONS—Four to six mind-stretching questions that challenge students to a new level of depth and integration.

STEP 4
MOVING OUT

This final step leads students out into their world with specific challenges to apply at school, at home and with their friends through three options based on your students' growth potential:

LIGHT THE FIRE—For junior highers who may or may not be Christians and need easily accessible application ideas.

FIRED UP—For students who are definitely Christians and are ready for more intense application ideas.

SPREAD THE FIRE—A special evangelism application idea for students with a passion to see others come to know Christ.

OTHER IMPORTANT MOVING PARTS

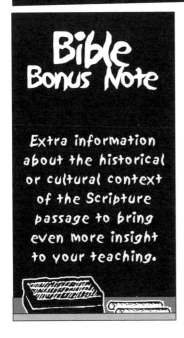

Bible Bonus Note

Extra information about the historical or cultural context of the Scripture passage to bring even more insight to your teaching.

Youth Leader Tip

Suggestions, options and/or other useful information to make your life easier or at least more interesting!

Devotions in Motion
WEEK FIVE: GRACE

Four devotionals for each session to keep the big idea moving through your junior highers' lives all week long.

ON THE MOVE—An appealing, easy-to-read handout you can give your junior highers to make sure they learn to take responsibility for their actions.

Dedication

To my sisters,
Terry and Luna,
The best
friends a girl
could have; and
To my lifelong
buddies, Lisa and
Nancy.

In memory of
Drew Helms, an
instant friend To
everyone he met.

Contributor

Natalie Chenault, author
of The student devotionals,
enjoys diet soda and pud-
ding cups. She attends
Eastern College and loves
hanging out with junior
highers. She hopes To
appear on Jeopardy! one
day.

It's Your Move

Junior Highers and Friends

Why Talk with Junior Highers About Friends?

Because it's who they are! It's a core issue in their world. When puberty hits, life changes. I know this is an obvious, oversimplified statement, but it's really the understatement of the century for young teens.

Life for junior highers is all about change. They're a bundle of physical, emotional, mental, spiritual and relational changes. The world of a young teen is expanding, both as a result of these changes and from attending a school that now draws from a region rather than the local neighborhood. With this personal world expansion comes new friendships, formed around common interests rather than physical proximity.

So, why talk to junior highers about friends? Because there aren't many things more important to junior highers than friendship. And because their identities are just beginning to form, junior highers need to understand the dynamics of true friendship.

How to Speak with Junior Highers About Friends

The subject of friends is so broad—there are a hundred different sessions you could teach, and most junior highers aren't interested in a 100-week teaching series! Here's a handful of things that are good for junior highers to understand:

- **God cares about our friendships**. God's not disinterested. He designed relationships, after all. And He desires for us to have healthy, fun, supportive friendships.
- **The best way to have good friendships is to be a good friend.** This sounds a bit cliché, I know, but it's a very true statement, and young teens often miss this point. They can be in a friendship for completely selfish reasons, treat a friend with disrespect and be bossy, and *still* wonder why it's not a good friendship.
- **Friendships often change as you grow up.** It's OK—even normal—for students to experience changes in their friendships when they move from childhood to their teenage years. Help them to understand that it's not necessarily a failed friendship if they don't still hit it off with their best friend from second grade.
- **Everyone is lonely sometimes.** The biggest friendship issue for some of the students in your group will be that they have no friends. Sometimes this is only a false perception; but sometimes it is the true reality. Help them understand that they aren't freaks or losers. It's tough to develop good friends, and everyone goes through times in life when they have fewer friends than they would like.

Enjoy speaking with your junior highers about friends. It's one of those rare subjects they will show some interest in!

—Kara Eckmann Powell

Pulse Friends

The Big Idea

Challenging one another by asking hard questions builds friendships.

Session Aims

In this session you will guide students to:

- Learn about the strong friendship between Jonathan and David that challenged them both to think and grow;
- Feel the need to build friendships that will challenge them to think and grow;
- Act by identifying at least one friendship that has the potential of helping them grow.

The Biggest Verse

"Then David fled from Naioth at Ramah and went to Jonathan and asked, 'What have I done? What is my crime? How have I wronged your father, that he is trying to take my life?'" 1 Samuel 20:1

Other Important Verses

1 Samuel 18:7,8; 20:1-4; Proverbs 12:15; Mark 8:27-30; Luke 15:7

Building Friendships

STEP
MOVING IN

This step illustrates that friends come in different shapes and sizes.

Option 1  Move It

You'll need Just this book!

Greet students and explain that you're going to start this new series on friendship by playing Go to the Wall. Everyone needs to stand in the center of the room. (It's best to play this in a room that's not too filled with furniture: perhaps another classroom as opposed to the youth room that may be filled with folding chairs and the refreshment table still covered with remnants of last week's donuts.)

Tell students you're going to call out four types of food and they need to listen to see which they like the most. As you call out the types of food, assign a wall for each one and tell students that they need to go to that wall. For instance, you might say: **If you like Mexican food, go to that wall; Chinese, go stand at that wall; Italian, go to that wall; and if you prefer Mom's home cookin', go to that wall.**

Next, do the same with vacations by asking students which **vacation location** they would prefer: a tropical beach; a cabin in the mountains; a Paris hotel; an amusement park in Orlando.

Continue the activity with other choices:

    Music styles: country, ska, rock 'n' roll, rap or pop;

    Cars: the new VW Bug, Mercedes convertible, Chevy Blazer or Porsche;

    Fast food: McDonalds, Taco Bell, Subway or Burger King;

    Movies: drama, adventure, science fiction, comedy or horror.

You can add to or change the lists to fit your group.

You'll find that students will enjoy the decision making and have fun being able to choose whatever they want. They'll also be surprised to see who else in their group ends up at the same wall with them—and who doesn't.

When you're finished, invite students to take their places and ask: **Did anyone feel left out when you went to a wall and some of your friends were at a different one? Was anyone surprised by the decisions of others? Did any two people here go to all of the same walls together?**

Explain: **Just as we have different tastes in food, restaurants, cars and music, we often enjoy hanging out with different kinds of friends. There are friends we have that make us laugh and let us goof off; we have friends for talking and sharing secrets; there are "just-for-fun" friends for going to a movie and the mall with; some of us have those special friends that challenge us and hold us accountable for our actions; there are even "crying-together" friends. Today we're going to look at how close friends can challenge us by asking hard and sometimes uncomfortable questions.**

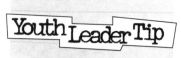

Youth Leader Tip

It's fun when, throughout the course of the group meeting, someone says something off-the-wall or funny and you sentence him or her by saying "Go to the wall!"

Option 2  Chat Room

You'll need A photo album that contains photos of you and your friends (past or present). If you have the time and technology, you might want to make overhead transparencies of several of the photos.

Greet students and explain: **Today we're starting a new series on friendship.** Have them sit around you and continue: **I have some special people to introduce to you.** Begin by opening your photo album and, one by one, point out special friends. Students will get a kick out of your hairstyles and clothes in the older pictures—let them have fun with it!

Share short stories of experiences you've had with your friends, making sure to point out how each one of them added to your life and growth as a Christian. Explain: **All through my life I've had different friends who've met different needs. Some of my most important relationships have been with friends who I haven't always agreed with, but who cared enough to dare me to grow up. Today we're going to look at how close friends can challenge us by asking hard and sometimes uncomfortable questions.**

Option 3  Fun and Games

You'll need Copies of "Word Up" (p. 21), a bell or buzzer, a watch with a second indicator and 3x5-inch index cards. If you're into prizes, you might want to prepare something for the winning team.

Ahead of time, cut apart the cards in the "Word Up" handout.

Greet students and explain that the topic of this new series is friendship. Next, divide the group into two teams. If the numbers work out equally, dividing the group into girls and guys can make for fun, healthy competition. This game is similar to Charades except that you talk! The girls' team needs to choose someone to go first, and then *only* that girl is shown a card with a main word written on it in all uppercase letters. This main word is the word that she has to try to get her team to say by using verbal clues, including words, phrases or sentences. Also listed on the card are words that she *cannot* use while trying to get her

team members to guess the main word.

The first team member has 20 seconds to get her team to guess the word. If she succeeds, then the next girl on the team gets a card and tries to do the same thing with a different word in 20 seconds or less.

If the first team cannot do it in 20 seconds, the guys' team goes next, repeating the process. Once the second team fails to guess a word within 20 seconds, it's the first team's turn again. As the leader, you need to watch the card closely and listen to the hints being given to the teams. If "forbidden" words are used, ring the bell or buzz the buzzer, and the point and the turn goes to the other team.

After about five minutes or after all the words have been guessed, invite students back to their places and explain: **As you can see, saying the wrong words is often very easy to do. Saying the right thing is usually harder to do, and the right words are hard to find. This is also true in our friendships. We often say the wrong words because we don't know what the right words are.**

Today we're going to look at how friends who ask hard questions and say words that challenge us can really be a good thing for us.

STEP  MOVING UP

This step introduces the way Jonathan and David's friendship helped them think and grow.

Option 1  Move It

You'll need Just this fantastic book.

Ask for four volunteers and assign them the following roles: David, David's arms, Jonathan and Jonathan's arms. Explain: **The Bible is full of stories about all kinds of friendships, and we're going to read a portion from probably the most famous friendship in all of the Old Testament.**

Instruct the volunteers that they will be acting out a short passage. The two students playing David and Jonathan will simply repeat what you (as the narrator) read, but the volunteers playing their arms should act with exaggerated animation in keeping with these particular verbs: "exclaimed," "protested," "fumed" and "begged." The funny and sometimes hilarious catch is that David and Jonathan must hold their hands behind their back while the two volunteers playing their arms stand behind them and slip their arms through to the front to gesture as their talking partner repeats the scripture. (**Note:** Giving the volunteers a few moments of rehearsal might help in making the delivery more creative and lively.)

Next, read the following script adapted from 1 Samuel 20:1-4, making sure to pause long enough to give the arms time to act out the emotions.

David exclaimed: (pause) **"What have I done? Why is your father so determined to kill me?"**

Jonathan protested: (pause) **"That's not true! I'm sure he's not planning any such thing, for he always tells me everything he's going to do, even little things, and I know he wouldn't hide something like this from me. It just isn't so."**

David fumed: (pause) **"Of course you don't know about it! Your father knows perfectly well about our friendship, so he has said to himself, 'I'll not tell Jonathan—why should I hurt him?' But the truth is that I am only a step away from death! I swear it by the Lord and by your own soul!"**

Jonathan begged: (pause) **"Whatever you want me to do, I'll do for you."**

When you're finished, thank your Oscar-award-winning cast, especially the arms, for their creative input in helping demonstrate the way Scripture can come alive.

Explain: **Jonathan and David were the best of friends, and in this passage, David had to inform Jonathan of some disturbing news about Jonathan's father. Their friendship was put to the test, but it passed with flying colors.**

Read 1 Samuel 20:1-4. Discuss the following:

Describe what you think might have been some of Jonathan's emotions when David told him the disturbing news about his father. Anger, denial.

What do you think were some of David's emotions? Desperation, anxiety.

How is Jonathan's final question a gesture of his loyal commitment (see verse 4)**?** He was no longer defending his father and he wanted to know how he could help.

If students are open to discussing how they would have felt if they had been Jonathan or David, encourage them to share.

Make it clear that Jonathan and David's friendship was strong and special, but strengthened even more as they both took risks and shared the truth. David was the kind of friend who cared enough to tell it like it was, and Jonathan was the kind of friend who was loyal even through the tough times.

Transition to the next point by encouraging students to think of people in their own lives who care enough to speak the truth, even though it might hurt.

Option 2  Chat Room

You'll need Several Bibles, one package of unsweetened baking chocolate (found in your local grocery store's baking aisle) and enough "real" candy for everyone (chocolate bars). **Note:** Most unsweetened baking chocolate bars come divided in smaller squares just like a regular chocolate bar; make sure you get enough so that each member in the group receives a small square.

Begin by explaining: **We have just discussed the fact that we all have different types of friends and we share with them in different ways. Sometimes our most important friendships are built around difficult situations and hard times. Often those times are uncomfortable and sometimes they can be painful, but the friendship sees us through and even helps us learn and grow in the midst of it all.**

Next, break the unsweetened chocolate bar into enough individual squares for everyone. Pass the chocolate around and invite each person to take a piece but *not to eat it yet*. Once everyone has a piece, instruct them to put the chocolate in their mouths at the same time. Their responses should be simultaneous and similar: *Yuck! Ewwww!*

Apologize for the bitter shock, and as you pass around "real" chocolate, explain: **A friendship can be just like bitter chocolate. It seems sweet, but it can turn bitter and challenge you. There is a great story of friendship in the Bible that was laced with bittersweetness, namely the bitterness of trouble and the sweetness of undying friendship between two men.** Have students follow along as you read 1 Samuel 20:1-4 aloud. Explain that Jonathan and David were great friends, but this disturbing news had the potential of ruining their relationship.

Discuss the following:

What did David risk by informing Jonathan about his dad's hatred? Rejection, losing his friend, angering Jonathan.

What did Jonathan risk by pledging his loyal support to David? He risked his father's love and support, even his own life.

Did the conversation here in this passage seem sour or bitter at first? Yes. **When did it turn sweet?** When

Jonathan said, "Whatever you want me to do, I'll do for you" (see verse 4).

Explain: **The friendship between Jonathan and David was strong and special and was strengthened even more as they shared the truth no matter how hard it may have been for David to share it or Jonathan to hear it.**

Option 3  Pulse Points

You'll need Your Bible, a spool of thread (or ball of yarn), a small piece of gauze (at least one-foot square) and a small piece of closely woven fabric (at least one-foot square).

The Big Idea
A good friendship will challenge us to grow.

The Big Question
Do we have strong, sincere friendships?

1. Friendships should challenge us.

Read 1 Samuel 20:1-4. Explain: **In this passage, David confronts Jonathan with the painful truth that Jonathan's father wants to kill David. This is hard for Jonathan to accept, and he tries to convince David otherwise. In this conversation between the two friends, David helps Jonathan take a hard look at the painful truth, and Jonathan is finally forced to make a choice. In the end, Jonathan pledges his support and allegiance to his friend.**

Illustration: Take the spool of thread (or ball of yarn) and, holding one end of the thread, throw the spool (ball) to a student, then ask the student a question, such as "How are you doing with your parents?" Explain that this question is one that will help that person grow and think more about how to live right.

Ask the student who is now holding the spool to hold onto the string of thread that links you to him/her; then throw the spool to another student while you ask that student another question to help him/her grow, such as "What chores can you work on this week?" Continue this process with several students until you have a web of thread linking your entire group. Explain: **This web that links us was built because we asked each other some questions that really got us thinking.**

2. Challenges should strengthen friendships.

Hold up the piece of gauze and explain: **Friendships that challenge us to think and grow are usually strong friendships. Take a look at this piece of gauze, which is made up of all sorts of threads and questions like our own web. The gauze is pretty thin; you can see through it and probably tear it apart easily. Let's say the threads of this gauze represent challenging moments in a friendship. They represent those long talks and hard questions.**

Hold up the piece of closely woven cloth and continue: **Now take a look at this piece of cloth. This is much thicker and stronger. You can't see through it or pull it apart very easily. There are more threads to strengthen it. The same is true in relationships that challenge us and help us grow. As threads of accountability, questions and counsel are woven, the fabric of that friendship grows stronger. The more challenging questions we ask our friends, the stronger and more solid the friendship! That's because we learn more about others; we challenge them to do the right thing and create an environment in which they can ask us some tough questions, too.**

STEP 3 MOVING ON

This step will help students feel the need for friendships that will challenge them to think and grow.

Option 1  Chat Room

You'll need Newsprint, a felt-tip pen (or a white board and a dry-erase marker) and a blindfold.

Ask for one volunteer and have him come up to the front. Blindfold him and give him the marker. Explain to the group that you are going to write down a word and the students are to guide the volunteer in drawing a picture of that word by yelling out instructions—but not telling the volunteer what the word is. Be sure and tell them that the *louder* the better so the instructions can be heard!

Once the volunteer is blindfolded, write the word "house" (remind the group not to say it out loud). At your signal they should yell out instructions, such as "Draw a straight line across." Allow a few minutes to see how far the volunteer gets.

Let the volunteer see the results of his efforts, applaud his work and ask for another volunteer. Blindfold the new volunteer and give her the marker with the same instructions. The difference this time is that you will choose only one student to give the instructions to the volunteer. Write the word "car" and ask the instructor to begin giving directions. After a few minutes, remove the blindfold and congratulate both the instructor and the instructee on their fine piece of art!

Ask the first volunteer: **How did you feel when everyone was shouting directions at you?** Confused, frustrated, unsure. Ask the second volunteer: **How did you feel?** Guided, secure.

Explain: **We all need help in life and friends are the perfect people to give us that help. Now, it might not be that we will need friends to help us to do something like drawing, but we will probably need our friends around for more important things.**

The world is filled with all kinds of voices shouting different messages at us. It can be confusing and deafening. But when we need help and direction or maybe encouragement, the single voice of one friend can do the job.

Discuss: **When are some times we need advice or help from a friend?** When we feel lonely; when we're having family problems; when we're struggling at school. **What are some things a good friend might say or ask that might be pretty tough to hear?** You really shouldn't be doing that; how's your relationship with God?; you should tell your parents; you were wrong.

Allow students to ponder this last question. Try to avoid hypothetical answers and push for real experiences when a friend dared to confront them.

Read Proverbs 12:15 and explain: **The Bible tells us it's important to surround ourselves with friends who care enough to give good advice that will stretch us and challenge us even though it might hurt. This advice might even come from your youth leader. Ouch!**

Option 2  Real Life

You'll need Your Bible.

Introduce this step by explaining: **Just as Jonathan had David to tell him some harsh but important truths, we also need people in our lives who care enough to be brutally honest.** Then read the following case study:

> Katie and Natasha have been friends since the second grade, best friends since the fifth. Now, they are in seventh grade together. Their favorite topics of discussion these days seem to be boys and clothes.
>
> About two months into the school year, Katie begins to hear comments and criticisms from others about how Natasha wears "skimpy" clothes. She even heard someone call her a "flirt."
>
> Katie is hurt by what people are saying about her friend, but the harder thing is, she somewhat agrees with them. Natasha is dressing a little differently lately. She considers talking to her, but is too afraid Natasha will be hurt.
>
> Katie loves Natasha, no matter what she wears. She just doesn't want her to get a reputation and really wants her to know what people are saying so maybe she can do something about it.

Discuss: **Would you confront Natasha or not? Why? If you were Katie, what would you say to Natasha? How might Natasha respond to Katie's confrontation?**

Explain: **There's a great verse in the Bible: "The way of a fool seems right to him, but a wise man listens to advice" (Proverbs 12:15). God puts people into our lives to challenge, correct and confront us when we need it.**

If all we did with our friends was go to the mall and movies, we'd be poorer—both spiritually and financially! It's important that we allow friendships to develop to the place where we can ask hard questions and tell the truth even when it hurts.

Option 3  Tough Questions

You'll need Nothing, nada.

1. **Why is it hard to tell others something that they don't want to hear, even though we know it would be good for them?** We're afraid to hurt their feelings; they might get angry; they might not like us anymore.

2. **Why does it hurt to hear the hard truth about ourselves from those we love?** We want them to think only good of us; we want to please them; we know we are doing something wrong but don't want to stop.

3. **Why is it easier to build friendships around having fun instead of deep discussions and confrontations?** It's more fun and not as painful.

4. **Why is it important to build friendships that will challenge us to grow?** God desires it; if we don't, all we'll have is shallow and meaningless relationships.

5. **What if we tell a friend something that they may not want to hear but is for their own good, and they get mad at us?** Pray for them and still try to be their friend. Hopefully, in time they'll realize it was best for them to know.

6. **If we're not sure whether we should talk to a friend or not, is it OK to talk to someone else and get their advice?** Not usually, because it can easily turn into gossip. Sometimes, though, you may need to talk to an adult for advice on how to tell a friend something he or she doesn't want to hear.

STEP 4 — MOVING OUT

This step will give students an opportunity to identify at least one friendship that has the potential to help them grow.

Option 1 — Light the Fire

You'll need A lot of prayer and several Bibles to give to students who make a commitment to Christ during this session.

> **Note:** Statistically, approximately 20 to 50 percent of the junior highers in any youth ministry have not asked Jesus Christ to be their Savior and Lord. This step allows them to make that decision by describing the most important question that can help us grow: Who is Jesus?

Explain: **We've talked about friendships that help us grow, and we're going to conclude by looking at *the* friendship that can help us grow more than any other. It's our friendship with Jesus.** Read Mark 8:27-30 aloud, then explain: **Jesus asked His friend Peter the most important question of all time: Who do you say I am?**

Jesus is asking you that question, too: Who do you say I am? There are three ways to answer: Jesus is either a liar, a lunatic or your Lord.

Today you have the chance to answer that question yourself, just like Peter did. You might say that everything Jesus said and did was lies, or you might say He was crazy. But if you believe that He's your Lord, I'd like you to pray the following prayer by repeating after me:

> **Jesus** (pause for students to repeat), **I know I often do wrong things** (pause), **and I know I need you to be my Lord.** (Pause.) **Please come into my life** (pause) **and take it over.** (Pause.) **Amen.**

Explain: **If you prayed this prayer and intend to make Jesus the Lord of your whole life, the Bible teaches that all of heaven is rejoicing** (see Luke 15:7)— **and we want to rejoice with you. Please come talk to me, so I can give you a Bible and answer questions you might have about your salvation.**

Option 2 — Fired Up

You'll need Copies of "Growing-Up Questions" (p. 00) and pens or pencils.

Explain: **Now that we've talked about our need to ask our friends some tough questions, let's get even more practical.** Distribute "Growing-Up Questions" and pens or pencils; then continue: **On this handout, you'll see several questions you could ask some of the most important people in your life. I want you to put a checkmark by each question that you think you can ask someone this week.** The handout questions correlate with varied levels of adolescent spiritual maturity, so there should be at least one question that will work for each student.

After giving students a few minutes to do this, continue: **Now I'd like you to circle the one question you know *for sure* you can ask this week.** Close in prayer, asking God to give each student the courage to approach a friend this week and ask him or her a question that will help him or her think and grow.

Option 3 — Spread the Fire

You'll need Nothing, zip, zilch!

Begin by explaining: **Sharing with others about Jesus is tough, but if we try to be friends that challenge others to think and grow, it will come naturally.** Divide students by drawing an imaginary line through the middle of the room. Continue: **Students on the right, I want you to come up with a situation that would be tough for one of your friends, like if her parents were getting divorced or if he had just been caught cheating.**

Students on the left, your job is to figure out how this tough situation would give you the chance to ask a question or share a bit about who Jesus is, something that would help the friend understand about Jesus.

Once both sides are finished, switch and ask the students on the left to share the tough situation while the students on the right brainstorm how this could open the door for conversations about God.

Close in prayer, asking God to help us all know how to help our non-Christian friends grow toward Christ.

Word Up

SECRET
Whisper
Tell
private
Keep
children

FAMILY
mom
dad
brother
sister
home

COMPUTER
Type
internet
E-mail
mouse
screen

JEANS
blue
pants
wear
denim
legs

FILM
camera
photo
movie
produce
color

BOOK
read
school
write
paper
words

MUSIC
listen
CD player
cassette player
stereo
radio

SCHOOL
class
student
Teacher
learn
junior high

FRIEND
Time
pal
someone
buddy
Talk

CAR
drive
steering wheel
road
go
gasoline

COMMERCIAL
radio
Television
sell
jingle
buy

CHEWING GUM
mouth
bubbles
pink
Tongue
blow

BASKET-BALL
hoop
Team
court
dribble
players

MILK
cookies
nonfat
low fat
white
cereal

LAMP
light
light bulb
read
room
lampshade

CALENDAR
days
months
years
plans
meetings

Growing-Up Questions

Check out these important people and put a check mark next to any question that you think you could ask them this week.

My Parents

☐ What is one extra chore I can do this week to help you out?

☐ What is one thing you wish I understood about you?

☐ If everyone would drive the same speed, would all of the traffic jams on the highways disappear?

☐ What could I do to help us get along better at home?

My God

☐ How do you want me to grow this week?

☐ Who do you want me to tell about You this week?

☐ How can I obey You when I'm around my friends?

☐ What's the square root of 9,586,342?

My Friends

☐ How can I help you with your homework this week?

☐ How can I be a better friend to you?

☐ Is there anything of mine you'd like to borrow?

☐ How do you get your hair so clean and shiny?

My Youth Leader

☐ Can I wash your car? Better yet, can I take up a collection to buy you a new car?

☐ How can I help out with the youth ministry this month?

☐ How can I be praying for you and your family?

Devotions in Motion

WEEK ONE: BUILDING FRIENDSHIPS

DAY 1

Quick Questions

Flip to Proverbs 27:17 and get sharpened!

God Says

Imagine you're camping and it's time to roast some marshmallows. Oh, no! You forgot the wire coat hangers to put the marshmallows on! You find a nice long stick, but it has a blunt, thick tip. What could you rub it against to make it sharp?

- ☐ The lint in your pocket
- ☐ A piece of squishy gum stuck to your shoe
- ☐ A big hard rock
- ☐ The side of your nylon tent

I Do

Do you and your friends sharpen each other like iron sharpening iron or are you squishy-soft like bubble gum?

What do you think it means to be strong like iron?

What can you say that would help your friends to sharpen up today?

FOLD HERE

DAY 4

Fast Facts

Flip, flip, flip to Ruth 1:14-18 and read about an amazing friend.

God Says

Lydia was the most popular seventh grader at Flying Mongoose Junior High. She was the prettiest, most fun girl in the whole class and she made excellent brownies, too. Everyone liked her, especially her two good friends Angie and Cori and, of course, her boyfriend Jason the most popular guy in the eighth grade.

In the summer before eighth grade, everything changed for Lydia. Her boyfriend dumped her, she got a really bad haircut, and to top it all off, she and her mom moved across town and she had to go to another school—Tiny Dog Middle School. Lydia told Cori and Angie that she didn't want them to hang out with her anymore. Cori said okay and went back to the friends she hung out with before she knew Lydia, but Angie said "No way!" and asked her parents to transfer her to Tiny Dog so Lydia wouldn't have to be alone.

I Do

Sometimes being a really good friend means doing things that may not be easy.

Is there a friend you know who is going through a tough time? Call him or her and ask how he or she is and if there is anything you can do to help.

If you're going through a hard time, call a friend and ask him or her to pray with you.

Fast Facts

Flip To Galatians 6:1-5 and see what you should be carrying for your friends.

God Says

Andrew and Jared were friends at church, but They didn't hang out much together at school. It wasn't That They didn't like each others; They just hung out with different groups. Jared played on The school soccer Team and Andrew hung out with The kids on The Team and spent most of his Time with The skaters. One day, Andrew stood a few people behind Jared in The lunch line and heard Jared and his friends making fun of The lunch lady, saying really mean Things about her.

The next night at youth group, Andrew walked up To Jared when he was alone and said, "I heard what you were saying about Lunch Lady Lu Anne yesterday. I know you probably didn't mean To, but it sure didn't sound like stuff a Christian should be saying."

I Do

Sometimes your friends will Tell you Things That are hard To hear, and sometimes you'll have To Tell your friends Things That are hard To say. A friend might Try To Tell you a way you were sinning or you might feel God wants you To say something To one of your friends.

As you walk with God Today, ask Him To help you listen To your friends and ask Him To give you The right words To say To Them.

FOLD HERE

Quick Questions

Run, don't walk, To 1 Thessalonians 5:14-11 and learn how To build!

God Says

If you were going To build a fort for your little cousin in your back-yard, what kind of Things would you want To use To make The fort a strong one?

☐ A package of Pop Tarts, some straws and some paste

☐ Two graham crackers, a gallon of white paint and some peanut butter

☐ An old refrigerator box, some Two-by-fours and a heavy blanket

I Do

Every conversation you have with your friends can build Them and you, Too. When you speak with your friends, are you giving Them solid Things, like encouragement and wisdom, To build with, or are The Things you Tell Them silly or mean or sinful? Make it a point To be extra encouraging To all of your friends Today.

Pulse Friends

The Big Idea

Sharing our true and honest feelings with each other strengthens our friendships.

Session Aims

In this session you will guide students to:

- Learn that friendships are strengthened through trust and honesty;
- Feel empowered to be honest in their close friendships;
- Act by sharing at least one untold secret pain, fear or dream with one another.

The Biggest Verse

"And Jonathan had David reaffirm his oath out of love for him, because he loved him as he loved himself." 1 Samuel 20:17

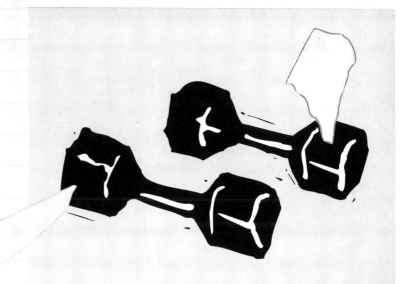

Strengthening Friendships

Other Important Verses

1 Samuel 20:5-17,41,42;
Matthew 18:15-17;
1 Thessalonians 2:8

STEP
MOVING IN

This step reminds us that we can't share our true feelings with our friends if we don't trust them.

Option 1 Move It

You'll need One copy of "Circle This" (p. 34) for every two students, a white board, and a dry-erase marker and a blindfold.

Ahead of time, cut the copies of "Circle This" into individual cards.

Greet students and explain that to start the session, you'll be assigning half of them to lie (they'll probably think: *Cool! It makes it legal when the youth leader asks us to do it!*) and half of them to tell the truth.

Next, choose one volunteer to come to the front. Give her the marker and blindfold her. Then distribute the cards to the remaining group and tell them not to blurt out what's on their cards. Half of them have the *false* diagram and half have the *true* diagram. (You decide which diagram is the *true* one and which is the *false*, but don't tell anyone.)

Instruct students to begin calling out instructions to the volunteer on how to draw the diagram that's on their card. The goal is to convince the volunteer that *their* diagram is the true one and to draw what's on their team's card. The key is for students to be very persuasive and strong in their coaching, trying to convince the volunteer that the other voices are lying.

Depending on the group size, the noise level can be deafening as students begin to yell out instructions. The volunteer doing the drawing is not allowed to speak. Remind the volunteer that even his closest friend might hold a "false" card and to be very careful in deciding who to trust.

Give this a few minutes. When the volunteer is finished drawing, take off the blindfold and reveal the true card. Let the winning team revel in their victory and thank the volunteer.

Ask the volunteer: **Was it hard to trust the voices you heard? How did you know who to trust and who not to trust?** Let them share and allow the group to add any responses.

Explain: **Sometimes we feel like there are different voices telling us different things, just like our poor volunteer here. There's our mom, dad, teacher, sister, brother, friends, youth leader, even the TV! Who do you listen to? The bigger question is, Who do you *trust?* Friendships are strengthened when we share our real and honest feelings with each other. But in order to do that, we have to *trust* that person with our real and honest feelings.**

Transition to the rest of the session by explaining: **Today we're going to look at how our friendships are strengthened by honest and deep sharing and how exercising the "muscle" of trust can help us do that.**

Option 2 Chat Room

You'll need Nothing!

Greet students and instruct them to stand in groups of three. The person with the longest hair is "It" in each group. Instruct those who are It to turn their backs on their two partners, place their hands across their chest "mummy" style and then drop—with legs straight—into the clutches of their trusting teammates. No bending of knees allowed! Invite them to do it again, this time with their eyes closed. Next, allow the person with the shortest hair to do the same and, finally, the one with the middle-length hair. On each turn, make sure to give a clear command, such as **one-two-three-drop!**

> **Note:** Try to be mindful and sensitive to any larger-sized students. If you see that a group may be mismatched (two tiny 12-year-olds and a much larger 14-year-old), subtly do some rearranging and gentle suggesting. Also be aware of your room arrangements and any objects that could cause injury. Don't become Accident Report # 312 at your church!

After everyone has had a turn, invite students to take their seats and discuss the following:

How did it feel to just drop? Fun, scary, weird.

Why was it scarier with your eyes closed? I couldn't see the room; I wasn't sure if my team was still there; being in the dark is just scarier.

Did anyone completely trust that their team would catch them? Allow for responses.

What would have made it easier for you to trust in this exercise? If it were my mom and dad; if it were a body builder behind me; if my team had the chance to do it enough times to build up my trust; if I could see where I was going as I fell.

Explain: **Trust, although it may be hard to do, is an important part in strengthening friendships. It's scary to trust our friends to catch us when we fall, but even scarier to do what we're going to talk about today: share our honest feelings with our friends!**

Option 3
Fun and Games

You'll need Blindfolds for half of the group members.

Ahead of time, plot a course for a Trust Walk, perhaps starting in the meeting room and ending at the front door of the church.

Greet students and explain that today they're going to do a Trust Walk through the church building. Explain that although they may have done it before, it's time to exercise their trust muscles again. Invite them to pair up and give them a blindfold.

Blindfold the tallest person on each team and instruct students that in this Trust Walk, no touching is allowed. The teams have 10 minutes to complete the course and the walk is done by voice instruction *only*. When each team reaches the turn-around point (the front door of the church), the teams should switch roles to come back to the meeting room.

Reward the team that finishes first with cheers, applause and a standing ovation and transition to the next step by explaining: **Trust is a big part of friendships. Today we're going to discover how it goes hand in hand with sharing our honest and deepest feelings.**

STEP 2
MOVING UP

This step teaches that trust and honest sharing strengthen friendships.

Option 1
Move It

You'll need Several Bibles, poster board (or construction paper) and markers.

Ahead of time, cut the poster board or construction paper into eight approximately 12x18-inch sheets. Write the following characteristics, each on a different sheet, in large print: "Loyalty," "Trust," "Love," "Commitment," "Faithfulness," "Communication," "Respect" and "Kindness."

Ask nine volunteers to come forward and give eight of them each a sign. Have the sign holders line up (in random order) facing the rest of the group. Instruct the remaining group to work together to come up with a consensus regarding the order of importance of the characteristics when it comes to developing close friendships. The ninth

Bible Bonus Note

There's even more to David and Jonathan's friendship than meets the eye. In 1 Samuel 20:13, Jonathan's blessing to David, "May the Lord be with you as he has been with my father," indicates that God had revealed to Jonathan that David would become the next king. What makes this more amazing is that Jonathan, the current king's son, was expected to be the next king. Jonathan is such a good friend to David and believes in him so much that he is willing to put aside any of his own selfish interests to do what is best both for David and for the Israelites.

volunteer is going to play "Vanna White" and move the cardholders into their new places. Pick a guy just for fun!

When the group has finished arranging, have the sign holders sit down where they are, holding their signs in front of them. Invite the rest of the group to open their Bibles to 1 Samuel 20 and explain: **We're going to read 1 Samuel 20:5-17,41,42 to search for these characteristics in David and Jonathan's friendship.** Ask volunteers to read, and as they come to the verses where a characteristic shows up (see below), stop and ask the group: **Which of the words is displayed in that verse?** As they identify the characteristics in David and Jonathan's friendship, invite the person holding that card to stand and move back.

- Kindness (vv. 5-8a)
- Commitment (v. 8b)
- Loyalty (v. 9)
- Communication (vv. 10-13)
- Faithfulness (vv. 14,15)
- Love (vv. 16,17)
- Respect (v. 41)
- Trust (v. 42)

Once all the words have been identified, continue: **David and Jonathan shared some hard times together. In those hard times they grew to trust each other with their honest thoughts and feelings. The more they trusted, the more they shared; and the more they shared, the stronger their friendship became. Evidence of this is found in verse 17: "And Jonathan had David reaffirm his oath out of love for him, because he loved him as he loved himself."**

Transition to the next step by explaining: **Just like David and Jonathan, our friendships can be strengthened by trusting someone enough to share our honest thoughts and real feelings with them.**

Option 2
Chat Room

You'll need Several Bibles, a white board and a dry-erase marker.

Ask students: **When you hear the words "best friends," which two best friends at your school come to mind?** Let them throw out some answers, which will likely be the names of two girls. If so, make mention of it and ask: **Isn't it interesting that the model of friendship in the Bible is the friendship between two men? Yes, girls and guys do some things differently in friendships, but there are three things common in all close friendships: trust, honesty and sharing.**

Write the words "trust," "honesty" and "sharing" on the white board. Explain to students that they should listen carefully as you read the scripture and shout out one of those words as it applies to the story. Some may yell out two different words at the same time. That's OK because that means they're listening! Read 1 Samuel 20:5-17,41,42. If they need help, you might want to pause while reading the scripture and wait.

Explain: **The deeper David and Jonathan shared, the deeper their friendship grew. These guys didn't just share what they did last weekend and talk about who won the chariot championships. They dug deep and risked big. They were honest and real.**

As the division between David and Jonathan's father grew wider, Jonathan and David's friendship grew stronger. Sometimes it takes a crisis to bring two people closer. But we don't have to wait for one for it to happen!

Option 3  Pulse Points

You'll need Several Bibles, a pair of scissors, a spool of thread and a spool of twine.

Ahead of time, cut the twine into pieces, each approximately one foot long.

The Big Idea
Honesty builds trust, and trust strengthens friendship.

The Big Question
Are we willing to open up and share our lives with others?

Begin by explaining: **A piece of thread seems so weak and small, but there are three things you can do with it that will make something strong.**

1. Share the threads.
Pass the scissors and spool of thread around and ask each student to cut off a piece approximately one foot long. As they are doing that, read 1 Samuel 20:5-17,41,42.

Explain: **David and Jonathan were obviously close friends, two peas in a pod, best buddies. But it didn't start out that way. Jonathan and David's friendship grew as they shared "threads" of their lives, hearts, thoughts and feelings with each other. It probably started by sharing small bits of things, like one or two strands at a time.** Invite students to hold the thread in their hands and pull on it. Continue: **Try to break it. Pretty easy, isn't it?**

2. Make the rope.
Give a piece of twine to each student. Hold up the twine and point out that it is made up of several tiny strands of fiber. Explain: **Try to break the twine. Not as easy to break as the thread, is it? David and Jonathan trusted each other enough to faithfully add strands of honest feelings and sharing. The more we share and the deeper we dig, the stronger the friendship grows. It's just like adding strand after strand of small threads to finally make a strong rope.**

3. Weave the net.
Have students get into groups of three and tie their three pieces of twine into a triangle. Explain: **This is the begin-** ning of a net. As Jonathan and David shared their true and honest feelings, their friendship grew and often served as a kind of safety net for them. They protected, defended and encouraged each other when they were down. This friendship safety net was there to catch them when they fell. It grew because they took the time to add threads of honest sharing, make a strong rope of trust and create a safety net of comfort, love and friendship.**

NOTES

Reminder

It is illegal to rent a video at the video store and show it to your youth group without first having purchased a license to do so. A blanket movie license can be bought by your church that will allow you to show virtually any movie to your youth group or congregation for one year by calling the Motion Picture Licensing Corporation at 1-800-462-8855.

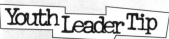

Youth Leader Tip

This can be a very intense time for students. Not only are they taking a risk by revealing their thoughts and feelings before their peers, but in doing so, they're encouraging each other to risk, trust and share. As youth workers we tend not to offer this opportunity to junior high students. Don't underestimate their potential for depth, honesty and vulnerability. Lead the way by sharing a personal story yourself.

STEP 3
MOVING ON

This step helps students feel comfortable about sharing honest and real feelings in their close friendships.

Option 1

Chat Room

You'll need A TV, a VCR and the video *The Horse Whisperer.*

Ahead of time, cue the video approximately one hour and 45 minutes from the opening Touchstone graphic to the scene in which the daughter runs to her room, slams the door and sulks on her bed. When her mom tries to talk to her, she clams up and pouts. Just when her mom gives up and turns to leave, she begins to cry and starts to let it all out. A touching moment!

> **CAUTION**
> Other parts of this video may be inappropriate for a junior high audience (even though many students may have seen the movie, there may be some whose parents do not allow such viewing), so you and your senior pastor and the parents will be better friends afterward if you cue the video to the exact spot.

Introduce the clip by explaining: **In this movie, a young girl is in a riding accident and she ends up losing one of her legs. Her anger causes her to go into a shell and her already strained relationship with her mother is now void of any closeness or conversation. Finally, one night it all comes out. Grab the Kleenex!**

After the video clip, explain that although this particular scene is played out between a daughter and a mother, this situation can relate to friendships as well. Discuss:

Why do you think it was so hard for the daughter to open up and share her real feelings? She was embarrassed, afraid, hurt, proud.

How do you think she felt after she shared what was really bothering her? Relieved, safe, closer to her mom.

Could anyone share about a time when you risked telling someone your deepest, honest feelings and were glad you did? What happened?

NOTES

Option 2  Real Life

You'll need Several Bibles, copies of "Pointers for Pete" (p. 35) and pens or pencils.

Read the following case study aloud:

Pete is in the seventh grade and a pretty average student. He goes to church and accepted Jesus as Savior when he was five years old, but last summer he made a solid decision to live for God and has tried to hang out with the right kind of friends who will have a positive influence on him.

Although he has good Christian friends, there is no one that Pete shares his deepest, most honest feelings with. His parents are great but they're, well, parents. Lately he has been struggling with feeling pretty unimportant and insignificant, especially in light of all of the athletic types and heartthrobs at his school. He's been noticing girls a lot more lately and is finding he's scared to death of them! These thoughts and feelings make him feel depressed.

There are a couple of guys from the youth group that Pete hangs out with, but he hasn't been able to share with them what's going on inside. He can probably talk to his youth pastor, but he really wishes he could talk to someone his own age, like maybe Jason. Jason is always nice to him and often asks how things are going. Pete gives the safe answer, "Great!" He just wishes he could say the truth, *I'm feeling really bummed, a little lonely and will probably never, ever date in my life.* But he doesn't.

Distribute pens or pencils and Pointers for Pete and explain: **You are appointed to give Pete three pointers for sharing his feelings and deepening his friendships. The three pointers need to start with "Always," "Never" and "Be." Use David and Jonathan's friendship in 1 Samuel 20 as a model of trust and sharing as you give Pete advice. Here's the catch: You can only give advice that you are willing to practice yourself!** Allow students to work in pairs and give them five minutes to write their "Pointers for Pete." Have several pairs share their answers. Praise and commend them on their great advice.

Option 3  Tough Questions

You'll need Several Bibles.

As you encourage students to dig deeper, begin by reading 1 Thessalonians 2:8: **"We loved you so much that we were delighted to share with you not only the gospel of God but our lives as well, because you had become so dear to us."**

1. **What do you think the phrase "share with you not only the gospel of God but our lives as well" means?** Not only do we need to share God's Word with each other, but we should also be willing to get close to people and share with them those things that life brings our way. It might be pain and despair or it might be joy and goodness. It also means just hanging out together every day.

2. **How can sharing our lives with people make us feel good?** It's easy to be superficial and put up a front, even when we're spending a lot of time with people. Sharing our lives with others can translate into taking risks by sharing more serious thoughts and feelings. This creates a trust and security that makes us feel safe and special.

3. **Given the current technology such as the internet with chat rooms, why are personal, face-to-face relationships important?** Our high-tech world of E-mail, voice mail and the internet has created an environment of easy isolation and anonymity, so we're not held accountable. Face-to-face human relationships are vital in the life of the Christian because God has placed within us a natural desire for fellowship and we can hold each other accountable to being obedient.

4. **What if you share something with someone and they turn around and tell the whole school?** Well, that stinks. Unfortunately, there are people (even Christians) who sin through gossip. The only way to know that a person can be trusted is to take the chance

Youth Leader Tip

This is a great exercise for those students who may not have developed close Christian friendships. It might be a step toward deeper and more serious sharing next time! Be sensitive to students who may not have many friends in the group, and when the time comes to divide them into small groups, be careful not to pair up a set of best friends with a third person. This exercise works best when you team up kids who aren't too familiar with each other.

by sharing little things at first; then when you see you can trust him or her, share deeper things. If your friend gossips about you, the first thing you should do is to talk to him or her and share your disappointment that your trust was broken and give your friend the opportunity to explain him- or herself. If the friend doesn't change, you might want to try again and bring a few others with you, as Jesus taught in Matthew 18:15-17. In the meantime, it would probably be wise not to share much with this friend until he or she has changed and earned back your trust.

STEP 4 — MOVING OUT

This step allows students to share some personal thoughts or feelings with someone else.

Option 1 — Light the Fire

You'll need Copies of "Do You Know?" (p. 36) and pens or pencils.

Introduce this step by explaining: **Right now, I'm going to give you an opportunity to practice what we've been talking about—honestly sharing our thoughts and feelings with one another.**

Distribute pens or pencils and "Do You Know?" and give students several minutes to complete the statements.

Next, divide students into groups of two or three and instruct them to share their answers with each other. After a few minutes, close the session by praying that God will give boldness and courage to students to share what they are thinking and feeling with their friends.

Option 2 — Fired Up

You'll need A package or spool of leather rope, embroidery floss, yarn, macrame string or any other suitable "friendship bracelet" material.

Explain to students that you'll be closing by looking at how easily this session on sharing in friendships can be applied during the next week. Encourage them to go deeper by sharing a secret ouch—a pain or disappointment they've kept inside—to someone within the next seven days.

Give each student a piece of leather, approximately eight inches long. If they decide to take the risk, explain to them: **After you've shared with your friend, ask her if she would tie the leather on your wrist as a sign that you shared. (Note:** Next week when you meet, make sure to ask who's got the bracelet on!)

Close by praying that God would give the students courage to share true and honest feelings with their close friends.

Option 3  Spread the Fire

You'll need Copies of "You're Invited" (p. 37) and pens or pencils.
   Ahead of time, cut the copies of "You're Invited" into individual tickets.

As you distribute invitation tickets to students, explain: **Today we've talked about strengthening friendships by sharing deeper. We're going to step in a different direction now, and I want to ask you to share something with a non-Christian friend. This week, think of someone you know who doesn't know the Lord and share with him that you go to church. Fill out this invitation ticket and put either the date and time of our next youth group meeting or our Sunday service. Try to deliver it to him or her in the next two days.** Close by praying for boldness for the students and for open hearts and minds of their non-Christian friends.

Youth Leader Tip

It's scary enough for adults to share their faith with non-Christian friends, yet we often expect students to do it without hesitation. One of the quickest and easiest steps students can take to reach out to their friends is to invite them to church. When visitors come to your church or youth ministry, your job is to make sure they feel welcome and understand what is happening. If they don't, they probably won't come back, and your own students probably won't want to invite anyone else.

Circle This

Pointers for Pete

Use David and Jonathan's friendship in 1 Samuel 20 as a model of trust and sharing as you give Pete advice. You can only give advice that *you* are willing to practice yourself!

Hey Pete!
  I know you're struggling with sharing your thoughts and feelings with friends. I'd like to give you some pointers:

Always

Never

Be

Do You Know?

If I could live anywhere in the world, I would live...

If I could live with anyone I wanted to, I would live with...

If I had all the money I wanted, I would...

My dream in life is to...

A goal I have for this year is...

My biggest fear is...

You're Invited

A gift for	A gift for	A gift for	A gift for
This is your free invitation to	This is your free invitation to	This is your free invitation to	This is your free invitation to
On	On	On	On
Beginning at	Beginning at	Beginning at	Beginning at
Ending at	Ending at	Ending at	Ending at
You'll be glad you came!	You'll be glad you came!	You'll be glad you came!	You'll be glad you came!

A gift for	A gift for	A gift for	A gift for
This is your free invitation to	This is your free invitation to	This is your free invitation to	This is your free invitation to
On	On	On	On
Beginning at	Beginning at	Beginning at	Beginning at
Ending at	Ending at	Ending at	Ending at
You'll be glad you came!	You'll be glad you came!	You'll be glad you came!	You'll be glad you came!

Devotions in Motion

WEEK TWO: STRENGTHENING FRIENDSHIPS

DAY 1

Quick Questions

Find Proverbs 24:26 and listen up!

God Says

You have to write a really important paper for your English class; it counts for half of your grade! The topic is hard and you work on it for a long, long time. When you are done, you ask some people what they think of it. Whose opinion would you listen to the most?

☐ Your Grandma Wendy: "It's nice, dear...and what pretty paper you printed it on!"

☐ Your brother: "It's a good paper...by the way, can I borrow 10 bucks?"

☐ Your best friend: "It's all right, but you need a stronger introduction and you had a few errors in grammar. Do you want me to help you with it?"

☐ Your mom or dad: "I didn't really have time to read it, but I skimmed it. It looked fine to me."

I Do

Can you depend on your friends to tell you the truth, even when the news isn't good?

Are you a friend that is honest, even when you have to tell your friend something he or she may not want to hear?

Pray that God will help you to be an honest friend today.

FOLD HERE

DAY 4

Fast Facts

Read Proverbs 27:6 and see what you can trust!

God Says

Linda and Karry went shopping together, looking for just the right outfit for the school dance the next Friday. While looking in the mirror after trying on a dress, Linda saw Leana and Trina behind her, the two most popular—and the meanest—girls in school. They oohed and ahhed about the dress and told her how she had to buy it and wear it to the dance. Leana and Trina had never even spoken to her before, and Linda was so impressed, she bought the dress without asking Karry what she thought.

Later, Karry said, "Are you sure about that dress? It didn't fit very well and I don't think the color is very good," but Linda thought Leana and Trina knew better than Karry. When she wore the dress to the dance, Leana and Trina came up to her and said very loudly, "I can't believe what you're wearing. That's the ugliest thing I've ever seen!"—and they both walked away laughing.

I Do

Sometimes we forget our friends are really on our side, especially when they tell us something we don't want to hear. Who do you listen to? Your friends or the crowd?

Who is one friend you can count on to tell you the truth? Thank God for that special friend. And thank him or her for being a good friend.

Fast Facts

Leap into John 8:32 and see how to get free!

God Says

John and Jake both tried out for the football team. Both made the first and second cuts, and at the final tryout, they were both told they didn't make the team.

John was so upset that he told his friends, "There was no way I could have made that team. The coach didn't like me from the beginning, and all the other guys trying out cheated. Man, I'm so mad. This is so unfair!"

Jake was really upset too, but he told his friends, "I just wasn't good enough, I guess. I really wanted to be on the team but I'll just have to work out more and try out again next year."

I Do

It's important to be honest with your friends and with yourself. What John told his friends just covered up the fact that he was hurt, but Jake's friends were able to know how he really felt, and because of that, they became better friends.

Do you tell your friends the truth about yourself, even when you are hurt or scared or sad?

What is one thing that is making you feel hurt or scared or sad that you could tell a friend about today?

FOLD HERE

Quick Questions

Read Hebrews 3:12-15 and decide if you're hard or soft!

God Says

Have you ever stretched the truth and said something to your friends like:

☐ "Oh, I've met Rosie O'Donnell" when you really just saw her at the mall signing books?

☐ "I totally know how to drive" when you only know how to drive a golf cart?

☐ "I've been to so many concerts I can't even count" when you've only been to two?

☐ "I love horror movies. They're so cool" when the only one you've seen gave you nightmares?

I Do

Sometimes it's hard just to be yourself around your friends. Although sometimes stretching the truth seems to be the key to getting people to like you, it isn't the best way to treat your friends. Honesty is a two-way street, and if you want to believe what your friends tell you, you need to be honest with them. Promise yourself and God that you will be truthful with your friends this week.

Friends

The Big Idea

Taking risks to serve each other deepens our friendships.

Session Aims

In this session you will guide students to:

- Discover that it's important to God that we serve others;
- Feel the satisfaction that comes from giving and helping others;
- Act by identifying one way to serve their friends this week.

The Biggest Verse

"Jonathan got up from the table in fierce anger; on that second day of the month he did not eat, because he was grieved at his father's shameful treatment of David." 1 Samuel 20:34

Other Important Verses

1 Samuel 20:24-42; Matthew 5—7; Mark 3:1-6; Luke 10:30-37; John 13:35; Romans 12:10; Philippians 2:3,4; James 2:14

Serving Our Friends

STEP

This step reminds us that serving others is a big part of a Christian's life.

Option 1  Move It

You'll need A brown paper bag containing 5 to 10 items (a coffee mug, a pen and pencil set, a hair accessory, etc.) purchased from a discount novelty store or picked up from your home or office. **Note:** You will be giving away these items, so if they are from your home or office, make sure you don't want or need them anymore!

Greet students and explain: **Today we're going to look at what it means to serve others. I'm going to give this bag to one of you and I want that person to reach into the bag and pull out something. Once you pull an item out of the bag, you need to quickly yell out a way to use that object to serve someone. There's a catch, though. Before I give you the bag, I'm going to name someone (science teacher, mom, dad, neighbor, the person who sits next to you in English, etc.) and that person is the one your object must serve! If someone else yells out a way it can be used to serve that person first, they get to keep it.**

Repeat this several times by giving the bag to several different students. Transition to the next step by explaining: **Now let's look at how serving, giving and helping are important steps in making friendships strong and lasting. So important, by the way, that the Bible talks a lot about them.**

Option 2  Chat Room

You'll need Four candy bars, several copies of the same issue of a local newspaper and your trivia questions, one of each for every four students. Make sure the newspapers are from the same day!

Ahead of time, search through the newspaper's Help Wanted section and come up with at least eight trivia questions, such as: *What is the last digit in the phone number of Minute Medical Tech?* or *How fast must someone type to work as an administrative assistant at the legal office of Galloway and Hays?* Don't forget to write the answers on *your* copy of the questions!

Greet students and divide them into groups of four. Give each group a newspaper and a copy of your trivia questions. Instruct them to find the Help Wanted advertisements and answer the questions. The team that finds each correct answer first gets the candy bars as their reward.

Ask: **If God were writing a Help Wanted ad, what do you think He would say about the type of person He wants to follow Him?** (Students' answers are likely to range from someone who is strong or someone who has a lot of money to someone who can bake cookies for the youth group.) Their answers may be a little limited or shallow. If students don't come up with words such as sharing, giving or helping, make sure you include them yourself.

Transition to the next step by explaining: **Serving, giving and helping are very important in the Christian life. Not only that, we'll see how they're important in making friendships strong and lasting.**

Option 3  Fun and Games

You'll need 10 pennies for each person present and a bag of miniature chocolate bars.

As students arrive, give each one 10 pennies. Introduce this new session by explaining: **This session focuses on serving and giving to each other in our friendships. We're going to start by actually giving to each other right now.**

Explain: **You have approximately 60 seconds to give away as many pennies as you can. There are only two rules: If someone offers you a penny you must take it and you can only give away one penny at a time. On your mark, get set, go!**

After 60 seconds, call the group back from chaos and ask who has the least amount of pennies. Congratulate the winner(s) for being so giving. If there is more than one winner, give each one a piece of candy—if there's only one winner, give him/her the whole bag! Collect the pennies and show your own giving spirit by donating them to the missionary fund.

Ask students how it felt to *give* and how it felt to *receive*. Allow for responses, then transition to the next step by explaining: **Let's look at what God says about giving, serving and helping our friends.**

STEP **MOVING UP**

This step teaches that God wants us to serve others even if it means risking our own comfort.

Option 1 — Move It

You'll need Your Bible, a roll of toilet paper, a rolled-up newspaper, three hats (the funkier the better), a small pillow or cushion, an overshirt, a backpack and one copy of "The Saga of the Good Samaritan" (pp. 49-50).

Ahead of time, practice reading the following script at least twice so you can read it smoothly in front of the students.

Remind students that they've been studying David and Jonathan's friendship as a great example from the Old Testament of friendship. Designate a "group Bible for the day" (either your own or one of your students') and pass it around, asking students to read aloud one to three verses from 1 Samuel 20:24-42 until the passage is finished. Once it is finished, ask: **What kind of risks did David and Jonathan take to serve each other?**

Explain: **It's not just in the Old Testament that we learn about friendships, but also in the New Testament. Jesus Himself told a great story about friendship in Luke 10:30-37 that we're going to look at together.** Ask for nine volunteers to act in a fun dramatization of Luke 10:30-37. Assign the actors their roles, give them the appropriate props and ask them to step to the side.

The instructions are simple: They should repeat what you say and do what you tell them using what you gave them. **Note:** Words in quotation marks should be repeated. Words in bold type are the narration. Whenever you see "pause" or other directions in parentheses that means to pause to let them say their lines or do the action. Read with dramatic inflection and lots of volume. So begins the saga of "The Good Samaritan."

After the drama is over, call all of the actors back up for a much-deserved standing ovation. If you have time, call them up separately and let them take a bow.

Explain: **This story—*slightly* edited—is taken from Luke 10.** Show students an open Bible turned to Luke 10 and continue: **Jesus used it as an example of helping others even though it's not the popular thing to do. It was a risk for the Samaritan to stop and help a Jew who was stranded and wounded along the road. He could have been attacked by the same guys who attacked the Jew, but he chose to take the chance and help out. Then Jesus said in verse 37 to His original listeners as well as to us today: "Go and do likewise."**

Transition to the next step by asking: **Have you ever taken a risk to help a friend or someone who is not a friend? Think about that as we move to the next step.**

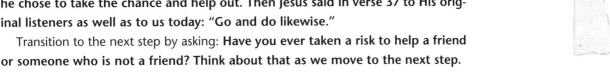

Youth Leader Tip

Sometimes those of us with small youth groups think we can't pull off certain activities because, well, we have small groups. This is where need breeds creativity! If you do not have enough people to pull off this skit, have the same students play more than one part. It can make for hilarious scenes and your students will feel important and involved. Who knows what inspiring young actors you might discover!

Bible Bonus Note

Often in youth ministry we make the mistake of acting as if the Old Testament and New Testament are separate books. The key is to understand how the Old Testament and New Testament relate to each other. In the New Testament, Jesus fulfilled many of the prophecies, promises and laws of the Old (see Matthew 5:17). He did not abolish them; He made them more complete. In the Sermon on the Mount in Matthew 5—7, Jesus shows that He's not abolishing the old laws, but He's giving their true and full meaning. Anytime in our teaching we can show the similarities between the Old and New Testaments, we will help make this clear to junior highers.

Option 2
Chat Room

You'll need Several Bibles, a TV, a VCR and the video *Forrest Gump*.

Ahead of time, cue the video approximately 53 minutes from the introductory graphic to the scene in which Forrest is trying to find his "best good friend Bubba" in the midst of a battle in the Vietnam War. Watch this clip ahead of time to make sure you avoid any controversial language.

> Other parts of this video would be inappropriate for a junior high audience (even though many students may have seen the movie, there may be some whose parents do not allow such viewing), so you and your senior pastor and the parents will be better friends afterward if you cue the video to the exact spot.

Set up the movie clip by explaining that Forrest Gump was a rather simple man who had a "best, good friend," Bubba. They met while they were serving in the military together. One day while the two are walking through a jungle with the rest of their patrol, they are attacked. Forrest is unharmed and he desperately tries to find Bubba and save him. Play the video clip.

After playing the clip, ask: **Why did Forrest go back and risk his own life to find Bubba? What do you think Forrest felt when he finally found him?**

Give an overview to 1 Samuel 20:24-42 by explaining that just like Forrest and Bubba, Jonathan covered David's back. David's life was in danger and Jonathan helped him escape. Jonathan risked not only ruining the relationship between him and his father in order to help out his friend, but also being killed or injured.

Invite students to read the Scripture in 1 Samuel 20:24-42 for themselves. Explain: **Friendship can be risky business when we really care about someone. David and Jonathan were so committed to each other that each would risk his life to help the other.**

Discuss: **What risks have you taken to help a friend? What risks have you seen others take to help a friend?**

Transition to the next step by explaining: **Serving others strengthens our friendships and lets people know we care. Jesus did the same thing for us by giving His very life! This serving thing is a big deal to God!**

NOTES

Option 3  Pulse Points

You'll need Several Bibles.

The Big Idea
Friendship involves serving, commitment and sacrifice.

The Big Question
Are we willing to take risks to serve others?

1. Taking risks shows we care.
Share the following story:

> A little girl was deathly ill with a rare disease and needed a blood transfusion. Her little brother was a perfect match, but when the doctors and his parents approached him about it, he was very hesitant and scared. He wanted to help save his sister's life but he was afraid to give his blood. Eventually, he decided he would do it. He didn't want his sister to die and she needed his blood to live. So he went to the hospital to have his blood drawn.
>
> As he was lying there on the gurney, he looked down at the needle in his arm, across the room at his sister in the other bed and up at the doctor. Finally, his eyes big as saucers and filled with tears, he asked with a trembling lip, "When do I start to die?"[1]

Explain: **The little boy was so afraid to give his blood to save his sister's life because he thought it meant he would have to die.** *Still* **he chose to help.**

We may not be called upon to give our lives to help others; however, we are called by God to give ourselves for others and their needs. There might be times when that giving or serving will be uncomfortable, maybe even painful.

As we've seen the last couple of weeks, David and Jonathan each risked their own well-being for the sake of the other. Their friendship was one of giving, serving, sacrifice and commitment. Read 1 Samuel 20:24-42 and discuss how Jonathan risked not only ruining the relationship between him and his father by helping his friend, but how he also risked being killed or injured.

2. Jesus took risks.
Explain: **The Bible is full of people who took risks for their friends, just like Jonathan did, but no one risked more than Jesus did for anybody, whether they were friends that He knew or not.** Read Mark 3:1-6. **In Mark 3:1-6, on the Sabbath Jesus was approached by a man who had a deformity. Jesus knew He could easily heal him simply by speaking the words. But healing was considered work and work was not allowed on the Sabbath according to the common interpretation of the Old Testament. Jesus also knew that the Pharisees, the "keepers of the law," were watching Him closely that day.**

If Jesus were to heal the deformed man, He would risk being accused of breaking the law and give the Pharisees more reason to want Him dead. What did He do? He chose to help. It was risky, unsafe and a bad move for a celebrity. It didn't matter—Jesus saw someone in need and had compassion for him. The ultimate example of this is Jesus' painful death for us on the cross, which is what gives us the chance to know God personally. What a risk He took for each of us!

STEP MOVING ON

This step helps students feel good about helping their friends.

Option 1  Chat Room

You'll need Copies of "If I Were a Tree..." (p. 51), pens or pencils and the book *The Giving Tree* by Shel Silverstein (Harper Collins Publishing, 1976 and 1997). This book is available in most secular bookstores, and once you get it, you'll be glad you have it.

Read *The Giving Tree* to students. If the group is small enough, make sure you hold the book so that students can see each picture. When the story is finished, discuss:

When was the tree happiest? After she gave to the boy.

If you were the tree, how would you feel after you gave and gave? Used, unappreciated; like I was wasting my time; or maybe good, useful, satisfied, happy.

How is *The Giving Tree* like Jesus?

Distribute pens or pencils and "If I Were a Tree..." and explain: **It's easy to feel good about giving when we get something back in return or when someone else notices. But the true test of friendship is giving even when it is difficult or hurts and even when no one notices.** Give students a minute or two to complete the handout, then have them pray silently for each friend they've listed.

Option 2 — Real Life

You'll need Nothing except this book!

Read the following illustration:

Katie and Lisa have been friends for a long time. They go to the same church and this year they're in the same eighth grade homeroom together. Lisa is an above-average student, but Katie has always struggled with her grades and has to work at them twice as long and hard as Lisa does.

Next Friday is a school party and both girls have been looking forward to going for weeks. They plan to go together with a few other friends. Lisa has a crush on Jerome, and a few of her friends told her they heard him say that if he sees Lisa at the party, he'll ask her to dance with him. She's so excited and can't wait to go.

The day before the party Katie calls Lisa in tears. Her parents have grounded her from the party because of her low grades. She has to spend the weekend studying for a math test on Monday. After about 10 minutes of "Oh my gosh! I can't believe this! I hate my parents," Lisa and Katie hang up.

As Lisa lies on her bed, she can't help thinking of her friend and her pain. Not only is Katie hurting, but she's struggling with her math work. Math comes easy for Lisa and she's all ready for Mr. Ward's math test on Monday. She realizes that if she spends the weekend with Katie to help her study, it would make a big difference in Katie's grade and they might be able to salvage part of the weekend and do something fun together. But, she doesn't want to miss the party either. This could be the big night for her and Jerome. Should she risk the chance and help her friend?

Discuss the following:

If you were Lisa, what would you do? If you were Katie, what would you tell Lisa to do?

How would you feel if you were Katie and your friend chose to go to the party without you?

How would you feel if your friend chose to help you study instead of going to the party?

Explain: **Developing important friendships can sometimes bring difficult choices to those involved, but our willingness to make choices to meet our** friends' needs over our own wants and desires will build strong foundations for our friendships.

Option 3  Tough Questions

You'll need Several Bibles!

Ask several students to read the following verses: Matthew 7:12; Romans 12:10; Philippians 2:3,4; James 2:14, then discuss the following questions:

1. **What is a common theme in all of these verses?** Helping others, putting ourselves second.

2. **Who do you think the "others" in these verses are?** Everyone, both Christians and non-Christians. Serving others is a great way to share God's love with them and possibly lead nonbelievers to Christ.

3. **Why do you think it is so important to God that we take care of each other and serve each other?** Jesus says in John 13:34 that the world will know we are Christians if we love one another. Loving, giving, helping, accepting and caring are all attributes of God, and He wants His children to be like Him.

4. **Sometimes it's hard enough to watch out for our own needs, let alone to put the needs of others above ours. Is God expecting too much from us? Why?** No, God knows the weakness that comes with being human. The love He shows to us makes it possible for us to serve others. It's the only way we can!

5. **What if we serve someone and they take advantage of us, like if we give a friend a dollar for lunch a few days in a row and he starts to assume we'll do it every day?** The key is to do what is best for him, and taking you for granted is not the best for him *or* you. Talk to him about it so he knows you still want to be friends—but as a friend, you want the best for him. First, find out why he is always borrowing: Do his parents not give him money? Or does he spend it on donuts on the way to school? Or does he just forget it?

If he forgets it or spends the money on other things, it's probably best to help him figure out a way to get his own lunch instead of taking your money every day. If his parents don't (or can't) give him money, maybe you could volunteer to make two lunches on some days and he can make two lunches on other days so that you can share and serve each other.

STEP 4  MOVING OUT

This step challenges students to serve a friend this week.

Option 1  Light the Fire

You'll need A copy machine close by, copies of "If You Ever Need a Hand..." (p. 52) and pens or pencils .

Ahead of time, practice photocopying your handprint onto the handout so that the image comes out in the middle of the page.

Tell students that you're all going on a little field trip to the church office. When you get there, place copies of "If You Ever Need a Hand..." in the paper supply tray. Invite each student to place one hand, palm down, on the copy machine, close the lid and make a photocopy of each person's hand.

When everyone has a copy of their hand, head back to the youth room. Distribute pens or pencils and ask students to sign their names on their own page, fold it in half and write down the name of the person they want to give it to. Encourage them to deliver the paper by the end of the day tomorrow.

Close the session by praying that God will help students meet the needs of others.

Option 2  Fired Up

You'll need One button of any kind for each student.

Ask students: **How many of you use a computer?** Explain: **If you're familiar with computers these days, you'll know that on most every window you're in, there's a button** that you can hit when you're stuck and have a question. What's that button called? The help button.

Close the session by explaining: **When we are working on the computer, we sometimes get stuck and need help. And sometimes we also need help in real life.** Challenge students to be that help button for their friends this week when they're feeling stuck, hurt, lonely or troubled.

Distribute the buttons, one for each person. Invite students to take the button and keep it in their pockets all week as a reminder to serve their friends. Continue: **At the end of the week, pass the "help button" on to someone else, pledging your friendship and challenging them to be someone else's help button.** Spend time in prayer asking students to pray for their friends by name and for God's help to serve them.

Option 3  Spread the Fire

You'll need A TV, a VCR, the video *Forrest Gump* and a roll of LifeSavers candy for each person.

Ahead of time, cue the video approximately 53 minutes from the introductory graphic where Forrest Gump keeps running back into the jungle to look for his "best good friend Bubba." He can't find him right away but finds others and carries them to safety. He finally finds his friend and brings him out. (**Note:** Be careful to screen for questionable language in the clip. Use the volume switch if needed to edit out any offensive words.)

> **Note:** If you've already used this clip in Step 2, Option 2, it's perfectly OK to use it again. There is power in repetition for the junior high mind!

Introduce the clip by explaining that you want your students to get a picture of true friendship in action. Show the clip.

After viewing the clip, explain: **Forrest cared about Bubba so much that he risked getting killed to save him. We may not ever have to risk our lives for our friends in the same way Forrest did. However, we may risk *their* lives if we don't care enough to share the gospel with them. You've heard the commercial slogan, "Friends don't let friends drive drunk." Well, here's an even more important one: "Friends don't let friends die lost."**

Distribute the LifeSavers rolls to everyone while explaining: **Each of you gets a roll of LifeSavers but**

don't open it. It will serve two purposes this week. The first is to remind you that God has appointed you as believers to be lifesavers to those who are lost. Forrest tried to save Bubba from dying in the battle. What are you trying to save people from? Remember that your witness and words could cause people to accept Jesus as their eternal Lifesaver.**

Its second purpose is that every time you help out a friend this week, offer them a LifeSaver (yes, you can have one too!). It may be an act as simple as stopping to say hi, sending them a little note or just handing them a piece of the candy and saying, "I've been praying for you." Your goal is to use up all of the candy by the end of the week (without eating all of it yourself!).

Close by praying for unsaved friends and for strength and opportunities to reach out to them with God's love.

Note
1. Adapted from Jim Burns, gen. ed. and Greg McKinnon, comp., "The Great Decision" *Illustrations, Stories and Quotes to Hang Your Message On* (Ventura, CA: Gospel Light, 1997), pp. 13, 14.

The Saga of the Good Samaritan

The Cast and Props

A bad man holding a rolled-up newspaper
A thief holding a pillow
A robber missing one shoe
A Pharisee wearing a hat
A priest wearing a hat and carrying a Bible
The Good Samaritan carrying a roll of toilet paper in a backpack
An innkeeper wearing the funkiest hat
A certain man (wearing a T-shirt and a loose overshirt)
A donkey (no prop, just a strong back!)

The Narration

One day a certain man was walking down the road, whistling as he went (pause), when all of a sudden, a thief, a bad man and a robber jumped out (pause while thief, bad man and robber enter) and attacked the certain man. They hit him (pause), and kicked him (pause), and when he fell to the ground they kicked him and hit him some more (pause). They took all of his money and they stole his clothes right off his back (pause)! And then they ran off like the cowards that they were, laughing like a band of hyenas. (Pause—if they don't laugh, repeat, "laughing like a band of hyenas.") And the certain man lay there in the road and moaned (cue him to moan painfully) and groaned (groan) in pain and agony. (Cue him to say "pain and agony!")

Down the same road a priest came along, praying as he went, "Oh God, bless me today." (Pause.) He came upon the certain man who moaned (pause for the moan), and groaned (pause for the groan) in pain and agony (pause—pain and agony). The priest said, "Why, look! A certain man." (Pause.) And he gently kicked him to see if he was still alive. And the man moaned (moan), and groaned (groan) in pain and agony (pain and agony). "He looks like he needs help" (pause), said the priest; "I should pray for him" (pause). Then he looked at his watch and gasped, "But not right now! I'll be late for church!" (Pause.)

And he went on his way. And the certain man moaned and groaned in pain and agony (more moaning and groaning—the certain man should have it down by now!).

Next, a Pharisee came down the same road humming a happy tune (pause), but his nose was so far in the air, he almost tripped over the certain man lying there (pause). And the certain man moaned...and groaned...in pain and agony. (By this time, your tone is a bit "yadda, yadda, hurry it up" when it comes to the moan, groan, pain and agony part.) The Pharisee said, "Why, look! A certain man!" (Pause.) He was disgusted and said, "He shouldn't be lying in the road like this! He's naked!" (Pause.) And the Pharisee stepped over the certain man and went on his way. And the certain man moaned...and groaned...in pain and agony (pause).

Just then the Good Samaritan came walking down the same road with his donkey by his side. (Pause.) He saw the naked certain man and yelled, "Oh, no! A poor, bleeding, naked, certain man!" (Pause.) The terrible thief, bad man and robber must have done this!" (Pause.) Just then, in the distance, he could hear the terrible thief, bad man and robber laughing like hyenas. (Laughing in the background.)

The Good Samaritan knelt down and took bandages (the toilet paper roll) from his pack. He began to bandage the certain man's head. (Allow Good Sam to roll a good amount of toilet paper layers around the certain man's head.) Then the Good Samaritan picked up the certain man (pause) and put him on his donkey (pause). And the certain man moaned (moan) and groaned (groan) in pain and agony. (Sound even more rushed as you wait for the moans, groans and pain and agonies.) He took the certain man to an inn and said to the innkeeper (appearing on the scene), "Here is some money. Please take care of him while I'm gone (pause). If he runs up a higher bill, I'll pay it when I get back." (Pause.) And the Good Samaritan paid the innkeeper to take care of the certain man and went on his way (pause). And that was the last we heard of the (here we go again!) moans and groans and the pain and agony. The end.

If I Were a Tree...

Imagine you were the tree in the story *The Giving Tree*. In each of these descriptions, you'll see what the tree did and what you could do for your friends that would be similar. Don't worry! We're not expecting you to grow any apples or branches. Write the name of a friend that you could give each gift. You can list the same friend more than once.

Play under my shade and swing from my branches.
I would invite _____ to
do this because he/she needs something fun and uplifting right
now.

Take my apples and sell them.
I would offer this to _____ because
he/she could use the extra help.

Take my branches and build a house.
I would give this to _____ because
things aren't so great in his/her house lately.

Take my trunk and build a boat to sail away.
I would offer this to _____ because
life's a little hard for him/her right now and he/she needs a
break.

Sit down on my tree stump and rest.
I would offer this to _____ because
he's/she's a little beat up lately and he/she needs a rest.

If You Ever Need a Hand...

You Can Count on Mine!

"Each of you should look not only to your own interests, but also to the interests of others."
Philippians 2:4

Devotions in Motion

WEEK THREE: SERVING OUR FRIENDS

DAY 1

Quick Questions

Hey! Go read John 15:12,13 right now!

God Says

What if your friend asked you to:

- [ ] Give up your favorite sport to tutor him/her in math?
- [ ] Use your allowance to buy him/her a pizza?
- [ ] Spend the weekend helping him/her move instead of going to the beach?
- [ ] Take care of his/her bratty little brother while he/she went to a dance?

Which of the following would you do if your best friend asked you to die so he/she could live? Would you?

I Do

Jesus loved you so much He gave up His life for you—this friend. What do you do for your friends? Do you ever sacrifice your time, money or your comfort to serve them?

Find a way to serve a friend today, like helping him/her to clean his/her room or do his/her chores or taking him/her to a movie.

FOLD HERE

DAY 4

Fast Facts

Flip to Philemon 6,7. Can you find it with your eyes closed?

God Says

Kelly and Mike were friends from school. Every day they would eat lunch together, and Mike would make Kelly laugh by making milk come out his nose, and Kelly would make Mike laugh by throwing Jell-O squares in the air and catching them in her mouth. After school they would walk home together, kicking the pebbles in the road and telling each other jokes. Sometimes they would hang out on Saturdays, but every Sunday Kelly went to church. Mike had never gone to church and wondered what it was all about, but Kelly never invited him.

I Do

The best thing you could ever do for a friend is show him/her the way to Christ.

Who are your non-Christian friends? Write their names down somewhere that you will see them every day and pray for them. Invite them to church, pray for your meals in front of them and let them know how in love with Jesus you are!

Fast Facts

Do you want to know what to do? Read Galatians 5:13 and find out!

God Says

At church, Nina and Carrie liked to goof off. They made fun of the younger kids, didn't sing during worship, talked during the sermon and giggled and poked each other whenever a leader tried to get them to behave. They thought that, because they were Christians, they could do anything they wanted to other Christians. Ellen and Lucy loved their church and liked to help out, but Nina and Carrie really distracted them. Ellen and Lucy asked Nina and Carrie to please be quiet and respectful in church, but they only got worse. Why did Nina and Carrie treat Ellen and Lucy as if they didn't really matter?

I Do

At church and with your Christian friends, sometimes it's easy to sit back and be served by others, never giving back. It's important to remember that being a Christian means giving to other Christians. Pray for your church today and ask God to show you a way you can serve there.

FOLD HERE -

Quick Questions

Look up John 13:1-5 and look down at your feet. When was the last time you washed those things?

God Says

Do you think you could do it if your best friend in the whole world asked you to:

- ☐ Wash his/her dog, Mr. Stinky?
- ☐ Sell all your things and give him/her the money?
- ☐ Clean his/her filthy bedroom?
- ☐ Run a 400-mile race with no shoes on?
- ☐ Clean his/her toilet with your favorite T-shirt?

I Do

When Jesus got down and washed His disciples' feet, they were totally amazed, because in those days, washing other people's feet was about as cool as washing gas-station toilets with your own toothbrush! Can you think of some totally amazing way you could serve your friends this week?

The Big Idea

Gossip can wreck and ruin friendships.

Session Aims

In this session you will guide students to:

* Discover how words can damage their relationships;
* See the importance of putting an end to damaging conversation;
* Act by speaking kindly about their friends.

The Biggest Verse

"Saul said to them, 'Listen, men of Benjamin! Will the son of Jesse give all of you fields and vineyards? Will he make all of you commanders of thousands and commanders of hundreds? Is that why you have all conspired against me? No one tells me when my son makes a covenant with the son of Jesse. None of you is concerned about me or tells me that my son has incited my servant to lie in wait for me, as he does today!'"
1 Samuel 22:7,8

Other Important Verses

1 Samuel 22:6-8; Psalm 12:1-8;
Matthew 5:23,24; 6:14;
Colossians 3:8,9,12-14; 4:5;
James 1:26; 3:5,6; 1 Peter 3:10

STEP

MOVING IN

This step shows students the power of the tongue.

Option 1 Move It

You'll need A tin of Altoids strong mints—extra strong would be even better. In case you're not familiar with Altoids, they're potent mints that come in a tin box and can be found at any drug or grocery store.

Greet the group and pass around the Altoids mints and invite everyone to take one and place it in their mouths, not because they need them, but to make a point. Some students might begin to make mention of how strong they are. Challenge them to try to keep the mint in one place in their mouth for as long as possible. It should be hard to do!

Explain: **How can such a tiny thing be so powerful?! That's the claim to fame of Altoids. Today we're going to talk about something else that is very small, yet very powerful. It's something we all have; in fact, it's in your mouth right along with your mint! That's right, your tongue.** Read James 3:5 and ask: **How can such a little muscle cause such great pain? Let's explore, especially now that we all have fresh breath.**

Option 2 Chat Room

You'll need Your Bible, a paper bag, a plastic bag, latex gloves and a cow tongue (available at most grocery meat departments; call ahead to make sure they have one in stock). This option is not for the weak of stomach! Store the tongue in a plastic bag, and before your group arrives, place it in the paper bag.

Greet students and tell them that you have something in the bag that will be the focus of today's session and invite them to guess what it is. Call on a few students to put their hands in the bag and feel what's inside and try to guess. After a few tries and a few guesses, tell them that it's like something that we all have with us all the time.

Finally, pull the tongue out of the bag and allow for a few *"Gross! Ewwh! Sick!"* comments.

Wear latex gloves while handling the tongue, and make sure students wash their hands after touching it!

While holding the larger end of the tongue (in the plastic bag, using latex gloves), explain: **Believe it or not, this is considered a delicacy. That means, some people consider it a luxury to eat it. Anyone ever have tongue tacos? Tongue sandwiches? Tongue stew? Cow tongue might not be on your menu, so we're not going to have tongue dessert after our meeting!**

Our tongues are such a small part of our bodies, yet they can do so much damage, or so much good. How can a small thing have that much power? Invite one student to read James 3:5,6. Continue: **I know this tongue seems big compared to our tongues. In fact, let's compare. Everyone stick out your tongue.** Walk around and hold the tongue beside a few of theirs. Transition to the next step by explaining that even though our tongues are much smaller than this humongous cow's tongue, ours possess much more power.

Option 3 Fun and Games

You'll need Nothing!

Greet students and introduce the new session by explaining: **Today we're going to focus on something very small but very powerful.** Divide students into groups of 8 to 10 people and have them sit on the floor in a circle with their legs crossed. If you have a small group, just make one circle.

Tell students that you're going to whisper something in the ear of one person in each circle, then that person will whisper the information to the person on his left, and the message must get passed around from ear to ear until it reaches the person who started it. Remind students that each person is only allowed to whisper the message one time, so they must listen carefully! And whisper!

In each group, whisper one of the following statements to the person who comes the closest to touching their tongue to their nose (if you need more than three statements, just use the same ones more than once).

They say that if a baby learns to walk early, it will probably not learn to talk early, and if it learns to talk early, it'll probably walk later.

Psychologists say that the normal person can have as many as 700 chances to speak every day and that a talkative person can use as many as 100,000 words in a day.

It's a known fact that girls talk more than guys, but the jury is still out on whether or not it's related to brain activity levels.

When everyone is finished, have the last person in each group report the statement he/she ended up with; then read the original message you gave to each group. You should have quite a discrepancy!

Explain that this is exactly how gossip works: **As it gets passed from person to person, it can get distorted, confused and downright untrue. Most of the time, it isn't something anyone else is supposed to know about in the first place! And it all begins with one little thing—the tongue. Today we're going to study this small but powerful thing that is able to cause both damage and pain in a single bound.**

STEP 2 MOVING UP

This step helps students understand that words can damage their relationships.

Option 1 Move It

You'll need A cardboard crown (available at most party supply stores or get one free from your local Burger King restaurant).

Invite two volunteers to come to the front of the room. Explain that they will be doing a scene from the Bible, but King Saul's throat is pretty sore from yelling all day. So he will need a voice double for this scene. One volunteer will play King Saul wearing the crown and the other will be the voice double. The voice double should stand directly behind the king and try very hard not to be seen.

Instruct the voice double to read 1 Samuel 22:7,8 slow enough so that King Saul can move his mouth as the words are spoken. King Saul should animate the scene by moving his hands and arms and use overacted facial expressions. It should come out looking like the worst foreign martial arts movie ever.

Begin by narrating verse 6: **"Now Saul heard that David and his men had been discovered. And Saul, spear in hand, was seated under the tamarisk tree on the hill at Gibeah, with all his officials standing around him."**

Bible Bonus Note

I know we think gangs are big today, but they were also big back in David and Jonathan's time. These gangs were based on family ties and tribal kinships that extended back to the 12 tribes of Israel. In 1 Samuel 22:7, Saul, a Benjamite, tries to strengthen his position with his own officials by stressing tribal loyalty. David takes a different path. Instead of trying to gain the alliance of his tribe, the tribe of Judah, he continues to trust God for his life and ministry, even when Saul is intent on killing him.

The voice double then reads verses 7 and 8: "**Listen, men of Benjamin! Will the son of Jesse give all of you fields and vineyards? Will he make all of you commanders of thousands and commanders of hundreds? Is that why you have all conspired against me? None of you is concerned about me or tells me that my son has incited my servant to lie in wait for me, as he does today."**

Thank your two actors and invite them to return to their seats. Then explain: **King Saul was jealous of David because he was afraid that David was getting too popular with people and would soon become king. By the way, that is eventually what happened, but it was God's plan, not David's. So Saul was after David, trying to kill him. And here in this passage, read so well by our voice double, King Saul was trying to turn people against David by tearing him down. Eventually, one of the soldiers came forward and confessed where David was. David soon experienced how words can be used to hurt, damage and even destroy people's lives.**

Transition to the next step by telling students that as Christians we should be doing our best to steer clear of

Option 2  Chat Room

damaging conversations.
You'll need Your Bible, copies of "From the Mouths of Babes" (p. 63) and pens or pencils.

Begin by asking students if they've ever heard this chant: **"Sticks and stones may break my bones, but words will never hurt me."**

Ask: **Who wrote this? What were they thinking!** It should say: **"Sticks and stones *might* break my bones, but words will *always* hurt me!"** David found this out the hard way.

Read 1 Samuel 22:6-8. Explain: **One of Saul's biggest weapons against David were words. In these verses we find him trying to turn his men against David. David soon learned that he was in a battle against anger, gossip, lies, jealousy and hate.** Saul's words hurt David deeply. In fact, when we read Psalm 12:1-8, we can hear him crying out to God in the midst of the lies and boasts that surround him.

Repeat the rhyme: **"Sticks and stones may break my bones, but words will never hurt me."** Next, distribute "From the Mouths of Babes" and pens or pencils and have

students divide into groups of four or five. Instruct them to rewrite this two-line rhyme, using about the same amount of words and similar rhythm. Give one or two of the following as examples:

"Friends and enemies might make me sad, but God will always love me."

"Stabs and jeers might bring me tears, but love will always dry them."

"People might laugh behind my back, but friends will stand beside me."

"The tongue can hurt when friends are curt, but I can rise above them."

After about five minutes, invite groups to share their rhymes. Praise everyone's efforts and transition to the next step by reading 1 Peter 3:10: **"For whoever would love life and see good days must keep his tongue from evil and his lips from deceitful speech."** Continue: **Now let's look at how we can do that.**

Option 3  Pulse Points

You'll need One dry pinto (or similar size) bean for each student.

The Big Idea
Gossip brings painful death to friendships.

The Big Question
Will we commit to getting rid of words that cause pain and hurt?

Open your talk by asking students: **Have you ever had a rock in your shoe? How does it feel?** Irritating, hurts, feels bigger than it really is. Read 1 Samuel 22:6-8 to illustrate how Saul tried to use negative words as a weapon against David. Explain: **Gossip is a lot like getting a pebble in your shoe. Here's how:**

1. It hurts.
There's nothing worse than being on a trail, hiking along, when all of sudden, you realize there's something in your shoe. It feels like a boulder even though it's actually only a tiny little pebble.

Gossip can be like that. There you are, minding your own business, when all of a sudden, you hear that someone has said something about you. It's not a huge thing, but it hurts. It's irritating and you want to get rid of it.

Distribute a pinto bean to each student and ask them each to stick the bean in one of their shoes. It will serve as a reminder of how words can hurt, just like a tiny little pebble—OK, bean. You might want to have them walk in place for a moment or two as you continue the talk to experience the discomfort.

2. It slows you down.

So you're hiking along with this rock in your shoe, it's hurting and you start to put more weight on your other foot. You adjust your step so that you're not walking on that tiny little pebble. And before you know it, you're moving slower and your pace is interrupted.

Gossip can slow us down, too. As it starts to eat at us, we find it's all we're thinking about. We talk to our friends about it, begin defending ourselves and accuse the other person. Before you know it, our lives have been interrupted.

3. It stops you.

Finally you can't take it anymore. You stop, sit down on the ground, untie your shoe and get rid of this tiny little irritating rock. Your hike is now totally at a standstill. Now your friends have to wait because you've slowed them down too.

Just like that irritating little pebble can interrupt a simple stroll, gossip can easily stop a good friendship dead in its tracks. It can damage even the best of friendships. You can only go so long with the pebble in your shoe—or the gossip—then it has to removed.

Close by explaining: **The best way to stop gossip? Do what you'd do to get rid of a pebble in your shoe; take it out and throw it away. The Bible says, "But now you must rid yourselves of all such things as these: anger, rage, malice, slander and filthy language from your lips" (Colossians 3:8). Let's remember the pain gossip causes and do our best not to place it in someone else's life.**

At this point you can have the students remove the pinto beans from their shoes or you might have them keep it there through the rest of the meeting as a reminder of the pain of damaging words.

STEP 3
MOVING ON

This step encourages students to end damaging conversations.

Option 1

Chat Room

You'll need A TV, a VCR, the video *Home Alone*, copies of "Home Alone, Too?" (p. 64) and pens or pencils.

Ahead of time, cue the video approximately one hour and seven minutes from the opening Twentieth Century Fox graphic to the scene in which Kevin is sitting in the church with the old man who lives on his street. They're having a conversation about family and how unkind words spoken in the past have damaged their relationships. The eight-year-old Kevin offers some great advice to his older neighbor.

Begin the session by viewing the video clip, then distribute pens or pencils and "Home Alone, Too?" and invite students to divide into groups of three to complete the statements on the handout. Give them several minutes to work on it and develop their own discussion. Transition to the next step by clarifying: **Sometimes in relationships, both parties are guilty and *someone* needs to be the big person and make the first move to say "I'm sorry." This next step might help us figure out how.**

Note: For further help in how to say you're sorry, refer to the student article "How to Say You're Sorry to God and Your Friends" on pages 95-96.

NOTES

Option 2  Real Life

You'll need Nothing!

Read the following story aloud:

Ken and Courtney have attended the same church since they were both four years old. They're good friends and have a lot of history together. At school, Courtney has a crush on a guy named Scott. He's pretty popular and a ton of girls like him. Ken doesn't know Scott very well, but he does know he has a reputation of "going too far" with a few girls. Ken has even heard him brag about it in the locker room during P. E. class.

One day, Ken was standing at his locker with a few friends when Scott came up and started to brag about how he and Courtney got hot and heavy after the game last Friday night. Ken immediately remembered, though, that his mom drove him and Courtney to the youth group pizza party right after the game. Kevin was just about to say something, but all of the guys began to congratulate Scott, giving him high fives and cheering him on. Ken's mouth froze and he couldn't say a thing.

Discuss:

How would you feel if you were Courtney and found out Ken didn't say anything?

Was Ken just as guilty as Scott?

What are some things that Ken could say or do to stop the gossip here? What would you do if you were Ken?

How does it make you feel when others defend you?

Explain: **It's often hard to know what to say right when you're hearing something like Ken heard about Courtney. That's why we're talking about it ahead of time.** If you have time, you may want to role-play some situations to help students prepare for what they face with their friends. Some sample situations might be:

• Brad starts a rumor that Davison stole Billy's skateboard, and Sean, who knows that Davison is innocent, finds out what Brad has been saying.

• Nicole hears Erica telling all the guys that their friend Sharon looked lame in her bathing suit.

Transition to the next step by explaining: **In order to have a friend, we have to be a friend. It might mean that we put an end to gossip by talking kindly about our friends and not joining in on damaging conversations—even if we risk looking bad or being singled out.**

Option 3  Tough Questions

You'll need Your Bible, an overhead projector, transparency and pen (or a white board and a dry-erase marker or a chalkboard and chalk).

Ahead of time, write out James 1:26 on the overhead transparency or board.

Have students read the verse aloud in unison. Then discuss the following:

1. **What does this verse mean?** It means that even Christians make mistakes and can get caught up in damaging conversations about people. The cool thing is that God forgives us when we're really, really sorry. However, if we continue to let our tongue cause pain and damage friendships, we need to take a hard look at our relationship with God.

2. **What does it mean in this verse when James wrote "he deceives himself"?** It means that this person thinks he's living a Christian life, but he's really blind to the damage his conversations are doing.

3. **As Christians, everything we say is evidence of whether or not we really love God and others. How can our gossip, jealousy and destructive words affect the non-Christians around us?** Others might think that Christians are no different from anyone else. They may think our faith in Christ is a big joke and doesn't mean anything to us.

4. **Isn't it more important to God that we don't sin with our actions, like by stealing, cheating or beating up someone, rather than sinning with our words?** No! Sin comes in several forms: actions, thoughts and words. Sinning with words can be just as bad as sinning with actions. God sees our hearts and judges our intentions. A person can intend to hurt with words just as much as—if not more than—physical blows.

5. **When is it right to tell someone else when a friend has told us a secret?** If the friend's secret is causing them or someone else harm, like if a parent is physically abusing them or if they're planning on beating someone up after school. You should tell an adult that you trust, such as a parent or stepparent, favorite teacher, small-group leader or youth leader.

Transition to the next step by explaining: **We are the only ones who can control our tongues. No one else is connected to that muscle. Let's look next at steps to help us do that.**

STEP 4 · MOVING OUT

This step helps students preserve their friendships by speaking kindly about their friends.

Option 1 · Light the Fire

You'll need Colored notepaper, a shoebox covered with wrapping paper (with a slit cut in the top) and pens or pencils.

Distribute colored notepaper to students as you explain: **Today we've talked about words and their power, and now you have a chance to use kind words to build someone up.**

Give students a few minutes to write a note of encouragement to someone else in your youth ministry. Instruct them to fold up the note, address it to the person they've written it to and place it in the special Encouragement Box (the newly glorified shoebox). You and your team of adult volunteers will deliver the notes after the meeting ends. Be sensitive to students who might not have as many friends and won't be as likely to receive a note from another student by having adult team members write encouragement notes to them.

If students really dive into this activity, you may want to keep the Encouragement Box out for several weeks—some junior high ministries have kept them out for several years!

Option 2 · Fired Up

You'll need Your Bible, a TV, several 3x5-inch index cards, pens or pencils and transparent tape.

Ahead of time, write the following words on separate index cards and tape them to the television screen: "lying," "anger," "rage," "malice," "slander," "filthy language." Then write the following words on different cards and put tape on the back of them: "compassion," "kindness," "humility," "gentleness," "patience," "forgiveness," "love." Be sure to have blank cards for the end of the activity.

Explain: **How many of you would feel comfortable if everything you said was tape-recorded, then played back for everyone to hear? Pretty scary. Well, whether you like it or not, everything that comes out of our mouths is a "talk" show. So, who stars in your "talk" show?**

Direct students' attention to the TV and read Colossians 3:8,9. As you read the words you've written on the cards, rip them off the TV. Give the index cards with the tape on the back to several students. Then read Colossians 3:12-14 and invite students with the cards to come up as they hear the word they are holding and tape that card to the TV.

Explain: **In your daily talk show, have you taken off lying, anger, rage, malice, slander and filthy language? Have you put on compassion, kindness, humility, gentleness, patience, forgiveness, love? Who stars in your show?**

Give each student a blank index card. Ask them to write down one way they can avoid gossip this week, using tips from the passage you just looked at. Make tape available so they can tape them to the TV set as a public sign of their commitment to putting on compassion, kindness, humility and all that other good stuff.

Option 3  Spread the Fire

You'll need Your Bible.

Begin by asking: **Did you know that some psychologists have observed that a typical person can have as many as 700 occasions to speak every day? And a talkative person can use as many as 100,000 words in a day!**

Our tongues are something we use to make a lot of noise with. However, when it comes to sharing our faith, often we're quiet. How lame! Think about it! When it comes to sharing the coolest thing that has ever happened to us, we clam up. In Colossians 4:5, Paul writes, "Be wise in the way you act toward outsiders; make the most of every opportunity."

Here's one way you can do that. At your school you probably have several fire extinguishers, and they're probably in a glass enclosure that is labeled "IN CASE OF FIRE, BREAK GLASS." Well, guess what? The fires of hell are raging and our friends need us, not to break the glass, but to break the silence and say something!

The next time you're at school, when you see a fire extinguisher, pray for one of your non-Christian friends. Ask God to show you how you can show your friend(s) His love this week. Then try to find the friend(s) and say hi, invite them to your church or youth group or tell them you prayed for them.

Challenge students: **Make some noise, break the silence, don't be lame.**

NOTES

From the Mouths of Babes

Sticks and stones may break my bones, but words will never hurt me.

Read the following verses from James 3:5,6: "Likewise the tongue is a small part of the body, but it makes great boasts. Consider what a great forest is set on fire by a small spark. The tongue also is a fire, a world of evil among the parts of the body. It corrupts the whole person, sets the whole course of his life on fire, and is itself set on fire by hell."

In light of those verses, work together as a group and write a rhyme to reflect how much words really can hurt!

Sticks and stones may break my bones, but words will never hurt me.

Read the following verses from James 3:5,6: "Likewise the tongue is a small part of the body, but it makes great boasts. Consider what a great forest is set on fire by a small spark. The tongue also is a fire, a world of evil among the parts of the body. It corrupts the whole person, sets the whole course of his life on fire, and is itself set on fire by hell."

In light of those verses, work together as a group and write a rhyme to reflect how much words really can hurt!

Home Alone, Too?

In the movie *Home Alone*, Kevin found out that because of some unkind words spoken many years ago, his neighbor was home alone, too.

What would you do if you were Kevin and his neighbor? The Bible gives great advice. Complete the following statements regarding the old man and his son and Kevin and his mom. Read the Scripture passages and use them to help you respond.

"Therefore, if you are offering your gift at the altar and there remember that your brother has something against you, leave your gift there in front of the altar. First go and be reconciled to your brother; then come and offer your gift" (Matthew 5:23,24).

If I were the old man, I would...

"Bear with each other and forgive whatever grievances you may have against one another. Forgive as the Lord forgave you" (Colossians 3:13).

If I were his son, I should...

"Therefore, as God's chosen people, holy and dearly loved, clothe yourselves with compassion, kindness, humility, gentleness and patience" (Colossians 3:12).

If I were Kevin, I really ought to...

"For if you forgive men when they sin against you, your heavenly Father will also forgive you" (Matthew 6:14).

If I were Kevin's mom, I should...

Devotions in Motion

WEEK FOUR: GOSSIP

DAY 1

Fast Facts

Read Proverbs 16:28 and see what's stirring.

God Says

One day Ginny heard from Sarah that Lara liked Moniaye's boyfriend, Garrett. She ran up to Moniaye and asked her if it was true. Moniaye said she didn't think so, but Ginny went to Garrett and told him that Lara did like him and asked him if he liked her. He told her that Moniaye was his girlfriend, not Lara. Then Ginny went to Lara and told her that Garrett hated her. Lara was really hurt so she went to Moniaye and told her that she really liked Garrett and didn't know why Garrett didn't like her. Moniaye, thinking that Lara liked her boyfriend as more than a friend, got really angry and told her she didn't think they should be friends anymore. Moniaye was hurt because she thought Lara was trying to cause trouble and Lara couldn't understand why Moniaye freaked out like that.

I Do

See how gossip can quickly grow out of control? And it only took one person to start the rumors! Don't hang out with gossips and don't be a gossip yourself.

Listen to yourself and your friends as you talk today. Are you gossiping? If so, ask God to take control of your mouth and ears. A great standard for gossip is if you can't say it to someone's face, don't say it behind his/her back!

FOLD HERE --

DAY 4

Quick Questions

Find 2 Timothy 2:16,17 and then look up "gangrene" in the dictionary. Gross!

God Says

What piece of gossip would be almost impossible to keep to yourself?

☐ The worst kid in school is about to be expelled.

☐ Your cousin is going to get married secretly.

☐ Your friends are planning on sneaking in to see your favorite band at a local coffee house without paying admission.

☐ Your sister took $10 from your brother's wallet.

☐ All the answers to the algebra test this Tuesday are C.

I Do

Gossip is totally addicting so don't get involved in it! Stay away from people that gossip and listen to yourself carefully to make sure you're not talking about other people or your friendships will suffer for it!

Quick Questions

DAY 2

Read 1 Timothy 6:20 and see where to turn!

God Says

Imagine that you're sitting with your friends at the lunch table. What would someone have to say to get you to turn off your ears?

- ☐ These french fries taste like rubber! Do you think they bounce?
- ☐ Did you see the earrings Jaime Tate had on? They were really cute!
- ☐ Andrew is so dumb. He got an F on the history quiz!
- ☐ Dana and I are going to the mall after school. She is so rich.
- ☐ Hey look! A green potato chip! Gross.

I Do.

Gossip is interesting and really hard to ignore, but if you value your friendships with other people, you will learn to ignore it. What will you do the next time you hear your friends gossiping? Join in? Walk away? Tell them to stop?

FOLD HERE --

Fast Facts

DAY 3

Look up Proverbs 17:9 and take cover!

God Says

Mattie failed her last English test and she was really scared that she would fail the whole class. Her dad thought grades were the most important things in the world and maybe that's why Mattie looked at Jill's paper during their English quiz.

After class, Jill asked to talk with her and she told Mattie that she knew she had cheated. If you need help, I'll tutor you after school." Jill promised. Mattie was really relieved. She told their teacher about the cheating, and although she got an F on that quiz, she got a B on the next one with Jill's help.

I Do.

Being a friend means helping out no matter what your friend has done to you. It never helps to tell other people how imperfect your buddy is, and that's a pretty quick way to lose that buddy too!

SESSIONFIVESESSIONFIVESESSIONFIVE

The Big Idea

Jealousy not only eats away at your friendships—it can eat away at you.

Session Aims

In this session you will guide students to:
- See how jealousy can divide and destroy friendships;
- Learn how to feel good about the successes of their friends;
- Act by praising one friend for his/her accomplishments.

The Biggest Verse

"Saul was very angry; this refrain galled him. 'They have credited David with tens of thousands,' he thought, 'but me with only thousands. What more can he get but the kingdom?' And from that time on Saul kept a jealous eye on David." 1 Samuel 18:8

Other Important Verses

Job 1—2; 1 Samuel 16:14; 18:5-16;
Proverbs 11:25;
Matthew 6:1,2,19,20; 23:5-7;
John 13:34,35; Romans 12:15;
1 Corinthians 13:4;
Philippians 2:1-4;
1 Thessalonians 5:11

Jealousy

STEP

MOVING IN

This step allows students to identify different ways to respond to the successes of others.

Option 1 Move It

You'll need Various popular magazines, scissors, several rolls of transparent tape and several large brown paper bags.

Welcome students and introduce this session as another topic on a "friendship wrecker." Divide students into groups of three or four. Distribute a few magazines, transparent tape, a pair of scissors and a paper bag to each group.

Ask them to look through the magazines and cut or rip out anything they see that might be something they want. Clarify that it doesn't have to be a material thing; it could be an ideal like being rich or successful, or maybe they would want someone's cute boyfriend or girlfriend. Encourage them to be creative. Instruct them to tape the images on the opened paper bag. After several minutes, invite each group to share some of their clippings.

Explain: **It's easy to look at what others have and want it for ourselves. This desire can produce feelings of greed, envy and jealousy. When these feelings creep into our friendships, they can eat away at everyone around.**

There will always be people in our lives who have more or better things than we do. The test of jealousy is not just a question of, Do you want it too? but more, Do you want them to NOT have it? *That* **is being jealous. Jealousy happens when someone resents an advantage that somebody else has, and although we think of it as something that happens in romantic relationships, it can happen in any relationship. And it has no place in friendships. It should be taken away and thrown out.**

Speaking of "throwing out," explain that without knowing it, they have just made "trash" of want and envy. Ask a few students to place these bags around the youth room to use as trash bags until they're ready to be thrown out.

Option 2 Chat Room

You'll need Enough Twinkies (or other treat) for each student.

Welcome students and introduce this session by explaining that this is another lesson on a "friendship wrecker." Declare that today is "Twinkie Day for Girls." Every girl present gets a Twinkie because...well, just because! Give each girl a Twinkie and invite them to eat and enjoy. The guys will certainly begin to complain and question this terrible unfairness.

Allow for a few moments of this, and then ask the guys: **Why do you think you should get Twinkies too?** Explain: **Your responses and feelings are very typical of most people. It's very human of us to want what others have, especially when we feel we deserve it. It's not easy to sit back and watch others prosper, succeed or gain popularity. Believe it or not, this happens in our friendships too. Why is it so hard to cheer on our friends and be happy when they're doing well? It may be because we are jealous. Jealousy happens when someone resents an advantage that somebody else has, and although we think of it as something that happens in romantic relationships, it can happen in any relationship, too.**

Transition to the next step by explaining: **Today we're going to check out the way our reaction to the success of others can make or break a friendship.** Before you continue, give the guys Twinkies too.

Option 3 Fun and Games

You'll need Lots of space.

Welcome students and explain: **We're going to step back to our elementary school days and play a little game of "Red Rover."** (OK, for some of your junior highers, it may be stepping back to last week.)

As a reminder, here's how: Find a large open space such as the church lawn or gym (or senior pastor's office?). Divide the group in half (**Note:** If you have more than 20 students, make multiple teams that can all play each other or create your own mini-tournament). Each team should hold hands and face the other team. The two teams should be standing parallel to each other and about 30 feet apart.

Flip a coin to decide which team goes first. The first person in the line begins the game by yelling, "Red Rover, Red Rover, bring (name of student) right over." The named student runs from his own team to the team that called his name and tries to run through the clasped hands of any two students. If he manages to break their grasp and run through, he gets to take both back to his own team. If not, he becomes part of the team that called his name and kept him from breaking through. After several minutes, declare the team with the most students remaining as the winning team.

Invite students to sit down, and ask: **How did it feel when you broke through the line?** Allow for some responses, then ask: **How did you feel when someone successfully broke through your line?** Discuss how confident some were that their hold was strong enough, yet the chain was broken and the team was separated in spite of that confidence.

Explain that in friendships, things can happen and words can be spoken that break up a seemingly strong friendship. Transition by explaining: **Today we're going to talk about something that often divides friendships—even strong ones.**

STEP **2** MOVING UP

This step teaches that jealousy can divide and destroy friendships.

Option 1  Move It

You'll need Several Bibles, a TV, a VCR, the video *The Princess Bride* and candy for prizes.

Ahead of time, cue the video approximately one hour and four minutes from the introductory Twentieth Century Fox graphic to the scene where Princess Buttercup and Prince Humperdink are having a conversation in Prince Humperdink's chambers about sending out the four fastest ships in his armada. Princess Buttercup then goes into a short monologue about the true love between her and Wesley. Humperdink is so filled with jealousy and rage that he goes to the "Pit of Despair" to kill Wesley.

Also, read 1 Samuel 18:5-16 several times so you're familiar with all of the details.

Introduce the video clip by explaining: **Prince Humperdink is jealous of the true love between Wesley and Buttercup; so much so that he can't stand the possibility of them ever being together. Let's take a look.** Begin the tape and stop it after Wesley's long moan.

After viewing the clip, explain: **As we just witnessed in this clip, jealousy can drive people to dangerous actions. In the case of Prince Humperdink, he was so jealous of the relationship between Wesley and Princess Buttercup that he wanted Wesley dead.**

Explain: **The Bible tells a story about a jealous king. His name was Saul. Saul and David were friends. Saul wanted David around and even gave him promotions.**

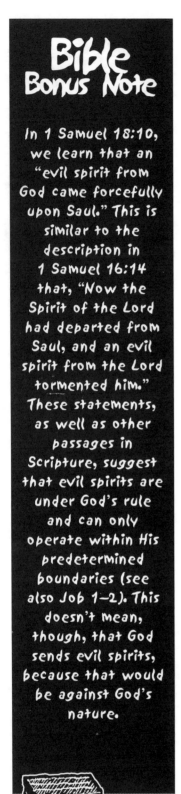
But then something happened—everyone started liking David better than King Saul. David was a handsome, skilled musician and a great warrior; in fact, he had just killed the Philistine giant, Goliath. Not only that, but the Bible said over and over again that "God was with him." People grew to love, respect and admire David and Saul didn't like it one bit. *He* wanted the attention and favor of the public, but David kept getting it. King Saul grew jealous, jealous enough to want David dead. Talk about a friendship wrecker!

Distribute Bibles and ask volunteers to read one or two verses from 1 Samuel 18:5-16 aloud until the passage is read in full. Explain: **I've studied this story ahead of time, and now we're going to play "Stump the Teacher." You can ask me any question that can be answered by the passage, and if I can't answer it, I'll give you some candy.** Do this for several minutes, then transition to the next step by emphasizing: **Jealousy can destroy and divide friends. One way to combat jealousy is to feel good when our friends succeed instead of wanting them to fail. Let's look at how we can do that.**

Option 2  Chat Room

You'll need Several Bibles and one or two school yearbooks from your students.

Ahead of time, ask to borrow a couple of your students' yearbooks (or use one of yours, if you dare!). Before students arrive, go through the yearbooks and note any pictures of groups or individuals that appear several times throughout the book. If you have more than 10 students, consider making overhead transparency copies of several pages ahead of time.

As students arrive, instruct them to sit cross-legged on the floor in a semicircle. In "storybook reading" fashion, show the yearbook, pointing out notable photos. If the person who owns the book is there, ask him or her to comment on the photos and the people in them. Ask: **How do you feel when you get your yearbook, look through it and don't find many—or any—pictures of yourself, yet there are lots of pictures of some of your friends?**

Share your own experiences of opening your yearbook for the first time, wondering if you "made it in." Explain that sometimes when our friends succeed and others pay attention to them, we might feel jealous. Yearbooks can be a reminder of who the school pays more attention to, and when it's not us, it hurts.

Explain: **There's a story in the Bible about two friends whose relationship was ruined because of a similar experience; one got a lot more attention than the other. At the start, Saul, who was king, liked David a lot. He wanted him around all the time and even promoted him. Saul called on David to play the harp for him when he was feeling down. Not only was David a great warrior, but he was a skilled musician, a quick learner, good looking, and God was blessing him. Eventually, the people grew to love, respect and admire David, especially after he killed the Philistine giant, Goliath. That would have assured him a huge picture in any newspaper, tabloid or yearbook! But *Saul* was king! He wanted the attention and favor of the public and yet David kept getting it. Everyone loved David, not just for killing the enemy giant Goliath, but for being a great guy. King Saul became jealous.** Invite students to turn in their Bibles to 1 Samuel 18:5-16 and assign several to read part of the passage.

Ask: **Why do you think Saul went from liking David to being jealous of him?** He felt threatened that others would like David more; he wanted all of the attention; David got credit that Saul wanted; he wanted to be the only one who succeeded.

Transition to the next step by emphasizing: **Jealousy can destroy and divide friends. One way to combat jealousy is to feel good when our friends succeed instead of wanting them to fail. Let's look at how we can do that.**

Option 3  Pulse Points

You'll need Your Bible, white (or yellow) and green play dough.

The Big Idea
Jealousy can work its way into a friendship and ultimately destroy it.

The Big Question
Can we rejoice when others prosper and succeed?

Pass the two colors of play dough around and instruct students to mix the two colors together, giving each student a few seconds to squeeze it. Have them pass it around until the whole group has a chance to knead and mix it. Explain the following:

1. Friendships can be divided by jealousy.
Read 1 Samuel 18:5-16. Explain: **Even though Saul and David were friends, David's successes began to scare Saul and eventually fill him with jealousy toward David. What was once friendship was now jealous envy and a broken relationship. If we allow jealousy in our friendships, it will most likely lead to the ruin of the relationship.**

Illustration: **Jealousy is like poison; it colors over a friendship until there is nothing left but hurt, regret and the memory of something that once was.** Point to the play dough and explain: **The white (or yellow) play dough represents the friendship; the green, jealousy. As jealousy enters the friendship, it eventually takes over, tainting it and changing it. It doesn't even look the same anymore. You see mostly green.**

2. People can be ruined by jealousy.
Explain: **Dwight L. Moody once told the fable of an eagle who was envious of another eagle that could fly better than he could. One day the bird saw an archer with a bow and arrow and said to him, "I wish you would bring down that eagle up there." The man said he would if he had some feathers for his arrow. So the jealous eagle pulled one out of his wing and gave it to the sportsman.**

The arrow was shot, but it didn't quite reach the rival bird because he was flying too high. The jealous eagle pulled out another feather, then another, until finally he had lost so many feathers that he himself couldn't fly. The archer took advantage of the situation, turned around and killed the helpless eagle. The point is that if you are jealous of others, the one you hurt the most by your actions is yourself.

At this point, ask for the play dough and divide it in half, with each half representing a separate friend. Begin to pull off pieces of the dough as you continue: **Saul's**

Remember that junior high students may not have as much experience with yearbooks as high school students. If you find this is the case with some students, use this option to give them a "heads up" of what's to come with high school yearbooks. It has proven to be an item that can bring feelings of insignificance, isolation and loneliness to the less popular students. It seems that high school yearbooks are filled with photos of athletes, cheerleaders the "in crowd." The rest of us usually get just the 1x1-inch portrait photo.

jealousy of David eventually led to his own despair and destruction. That is likely to happen in our friendships if we let feelings of jealousy eat away at us. And it will—unless we get rid of it.

3. Praise and encouragement can end jealousy.

Read 1 Thessalonians 5:11 and explain: **If jealousy is a fire, praise and encouragement are water to put out that fire! Instead of feeling jealous of what our friends are or what they have, rejoice with them! Applaud their accomplishments, encourage their efforts and praise their achievements. This is a sure way to kill feelings of jealousy.** Combine the play dough into one big clump and continue: **This play dough can also represent a friendship that is overcome with jealousy or one that is getting stronger. Just as it represented jealousy, the green can also represent words of praise and encouragement—which also work their way through an entire friendship.**

STEP

MOVING ON

This step will help students learn to feel good about the successes of their friends.

Option 1

Chat Room

You'll need Copies of "Complimentary Compliments" (p. 75) and pens and pencils.

Introduce this next step by explaining: **Since jealousy is a sure way to wreck a friendship, we should do what we can to avoid it or get rid of it. Learning to appreciate our friends and praise their accomplishments is a great repair kit.**

Ask for a volunteer to read Philippians 2:1-4. Distribute pens or pencils and "Complimentary Compliments" and give students five minutes to complete the handout. Next, have students divide into groups of three or four and discuss their answers. Transition to the next step by explaining: **Now you'll have an opportunity to try this out for real!**

Option 2

Real Life

You'll need A Bible.

Read the following story:

Reid and Luke are great friends and both serve on the student council. Reid was nominated to be in charge of coordinating the eighth-grade dance and Luke offered to help him in any way he could. Luke and Reid met a few times to discuss the details and divide up the responsibilities evenly. Between them, they came up with the theme, coordinated all the decorations, lined up chaperones, scheduled the deejay and made all the arrangements for the refreshments.

The dance turned out to be a blast! Everything ran smoothly and was the most successful dance of the year. Everyone was commenting on how much fun they were having and no one wanted to go home. Before the end of the evening, the vice principal called Reid up to the stage to publicly thank him and congratulate him on a great job. The whole school cheered him on. Afterward, Reid went to Luke and thanked him for his help.

Discuss the following question: **How would you feel if you were Luke?** After a short discussion, read from Romans 12:15, **"Rejoice with those who rejoice; mourn with those who mourn."** Reid *was* the coordinator of the dance and it was his job to make it happen whether he did it himself or asked for the help of others. In light of this, how should Luke respond to the attention and applause Reid received for the success of the dance?

Ask students to put themselves in Luke's shoes and give examples of praise and compliments that he could give to Reid, as well as encouragement that Reid could give to Luke.

NOTES

Option 3 — Tough Questions

You'll need Several Bibles.

Discuss the following questions:

1. **Why are we quick to feel jealousy instead of joy when others succeed?** It is our sinful nature that makes us think of ourselves first. Because of the fall of Adam and Eve, we are born selfish—more concerned about *our* well-being and prosperity than that of others. It is possible to be concerned about others and rejoice in their accomplishments, but it takes work. As Paul encourages us in Romans 12:15, we can "Rejoice with those who rejoice; mourn with those who mourn." But in order to do that, we need to ask for Christ's help.

2. **Is it okay to *feel* jealous about someone as long as we *act* supportive towards them?** Well, no, not really. Sometimes feelings are hard to control and it's easier to put up a front and behave differently than how we feel inside. But if you're struggling with jealous feelings, pray and ask God to change your heart and to even bless the person you're jealous of.

3. **Based on Matthew 6:19,20, how is wanting praise and attention like storing up treasures here on earth?** Wanting praise and attention for our actions or accomplishments is much like being rewarded for what we do and who we are. Jesus said that our reward will be in heaven and not to seek the praise of men (see Matthew 6:1,2; 23:5-7). Trying to gain honor and praise here on earth could make us lose out in heaven! We may earn the praise of others, but if we store those treasures here on earth, they will soon rot away and disappear.

4. **Proverbs 11:25 teaches, "A generous man will prosper; he who refreshes others will himself be refreshed." How can refreshing others make us prosper?** God created us and knows that giving to others and regarding them above ourselves will help us feel great! Being generous with words of praise and encouragement will bring us joy just as much as being generous with money or material things will.

5. **What do I do if one of my friends is jealous of *me*?** Try to be humble and show God's love to him or her. Make sure you encourage her and affirm any of her own special talents or abilities.

STEP 4 — MOVING OUT

This step helps students put their learning into action by praising their friends for their accomplishments and successes.

Option 1 — Light the Fire

You'll need Copies of "Certificate of Appreciation" (p. 76) and pens or pencils.

Distribute pens or pencils and "Certificate of Appreciation" to students. Explain that they have an opportunity to counteract any feelings of jealousy by giving praise and appreciation to one friend. Give them several minutes to complete the handout and encourage them to give it to a friend this week.

Close the lesson by praying for forgiveness for any feelings of jealousy and envy in our friendships.

Option 2 — Fired Up

You'll need Copies of "A Walk Through the Forest" (p. 77) and pens or pencils.

Distribute pens or pencils and "A Walk Through the Forest" and give students a few minutes to complete it. Then spend time to allow them to share their responses and give each other encouragement, praise and honor.

Close by praying for the friendships in the youth group and ask God to help students be givers of joy and approval rather than jealousy and envy.

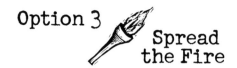
You'll need Poster board and several felt-tip pens.

Explain: **People come to Christ as a result of many different reasons. It could be that there was a crisis in their lives that caused them to seek God. Perhaps they simply searched high and low for peace and purpose until they found Him. One of the most common is that they saw others who seemed different, probably because they cared about each other and weren't petty and jealous.** Read John 13:34,35. **"A new command I give you: Love one another. As I have loved you, so you must love one another. By this all men will know that you are my disciples, if you love one another."**

Ask: **How does this verse relate to jealousy? How could we, in our junior high ministry, be so loving to each other that others would see something different about us?** Write their answers on the poster board. Answers may include things such as: not gossiping, being happy for each other, congratulating each other and complimenting each other. Ask: **How would this help our guests understand more about Jesus?**

Continue: **If you'd like to commit to do any of these acts of loving each other for the next month, please come up and put your initials next to that idea on the board. You can commit to more than one, if you'd like, but just make sure you only commit to what you can realistically do.** Give students a few minutes to do this, then conclude by praying that unsaved friends will see Christ through the way we love each other. Keep the poster board up in your meeting room for about a month to remind students of their commitments.

Youth Leader Tip

If you choose this option to close the session, allow for considerable time for sharing and perhaps even some unexpected moments. It's opportunities like this that can build, bond and help the group members to the next level of relationship. Also, be sensitive to students who may not be as likely to be mentioned by making sure adult volunteers share about them. It feels awful to sit and wait for your own name to be called, only to end up disappointed and discouraged when no one mentions you.

NOTES

Complimentary Compliments

Learning To give praise and appreciaTion Takes pracTice. This acTiviTy will help you pracTice The arT of complimenTing oThers when They succeed.

Your besT friend geTs asked To The dance by The cuTesT girl/guy in your class. You were hoping iT would happen To you.

You cheer him/her on by saying...

You and your friend sTay up laTe sTudying for The big science TesT. Your friend geTs an A- and you geT a C+.

You praise your friend by...

Your friend is running for class presidenT. He/she is geTTing a loT of aTTenTion laTely and you feel a liTTle lefT ouT. You hear some classmaTes Talking abouT how greaT your friend would be as class presidenT.

You supporT your friend by saying...

You and your friend audiTion for The big school musical. Your friend geTs The lead parT and you geT a small supporTing role.

You encourage and applaud your friend by...

Certificate of Appreciation

"Love is patient, love is kind. It does not envy, it does not boast, it is not proud." 1 Corinthians 13:4

Presented to _____
(name of friend)

for possessing the exceptional qualities of _____
(inner qualities or notable characteristics)

and for excellent accomplishment in _____
(skills, talents or abilities)

Signed, your friend _____ Date _____

"Love is patient, love is kind. It does not envy, it does not boast, it is not proud." 1 Corinthians 13:4

Presented to _____
(name of friend)

for possessing the exceptional qualities of _____
(inner qualities or notable characteristics)

and for excellent accomplishment in _____
(skills, talents or abilities)

Signed, your friend _____ Date _____

A Walk Through the Forest

Praise and encouragement can be like glue that keeps friends together. Try to identify someone in your group who resembles one of the following statements:

_____ is like a path—always pointing us in the right direction and showing us the way to go.

_____ is like a tree—standing tall, strong and firm no matter what happens.

_____ is like a cool stream—helping us feel better when things get dry and boring.

_____ is like a tent—making us feel at home.

_____ is like wildflowers—adding color and joy to our group.

_____ is like sunshine—lots of energy and always warm and giving.

_____ is like an open meadow—a calm and quiet spirit that helps us relax.

Devotions in Motion

WEEK FIVE: JEALOUSY

DAY 1

Fast Facts

Find James 3:13-18 and don't brag about it!

God Says

Will wished he could play baseball like Steven or be really good at science like Gina or play piano like Hope. Will whined and complained, constantly telling his friends that he wished he was like them—until they were all sick of hearing it. Instead of learning to do something like play the flute or dance the latest dance, he began to really dislike his friends. It's not fair, he thought, they're all a bunch of showoffs. What jerks?

I Do

Admiring your friends and enjoying the talents God gave them is fun, but being jealous is another thing entirely. It's easy to become jealous when you don't totally like who you are or what you can do.

Pray for God to give you peace and appreciation about who you are and to help you enjoy and encourage the friends He has given you!

FOLD HERE

DAY 4

Quick Questions

Go to Romans 16:17-19 and get ready to party!

God Says

Imagine you're at a party. The first person you meet is reading magazines, and as she looks through them, she comments on how this model has the perfect nose, that one has perfect hair and that model has a perfect body. How would you begin to feel about the way you look?

The next person you meet is a guy who is talking about a pair of $300 basketball shoes that he's going to get with lights and space-age materials and glow-in-the-dark soles. How would you begin to think about your shoes?

The next person you meet is watching MTV, talking about how if you don't dress like the people on MTV, you just ain't cool. How would you begin to feel about your clothes?

I Do

Do you think hanging out with envious people is a good idea or a bad one? If you hang out with people who are always complaining about how they don't have cool clothes or the right house, their attitudes will start to rub off on you and make you unhappy with your life and yourself.

Are you happy with who you are? Are your friends? Ask God to help you and your friends be content with everything He has given you.

Quick QuesTions

Read Proverbs 14:30 To find out if There's someThing roTTen in here.

God Says

WhaT is one Thing you would love To be able To do?

- ☐ Play baseball beTTer Than Babe RuTh
- ☐ Dance like one of The famous balleT dancers
- ☐ STop Time by Touching your index finger To your nose
- ☐ Be a famous acTor and win an Oscar award
- ☐ Sing beTTer Than any famous rock sTar

I Do.

WanTing To do someThing well is cool, buT when you focus all your energy on being beTTer Than someone else, ThaT person becomes your enemy. IT's really hard To love someone you're always Trying To outdo!

Do yourself a favor—don'T Try To be beTTer Than any of your friends. Thank God for puTTing Them in your life and be The besT YOU ThaT you can be!

FOLD HERE

---

fasT facTs

Don'T delay, buT check ouT 1 CorinThians 13:4.

God Says

Megan and JuaniTa have been friends since They were five years old and meT at Sunday School. Now ThaT They're in junior high, They've boTh changed a loT. For insTance, JuaniTa has a beauTiful singing voice and does solos in junior high and in fronT of The enTire church someTimes. JuaniTa also really likes To be a leader, so she joined The minisTry Team and now she helps plan bake sales and overnighTers and car washes. Everybody Thinks she's a really greaT ChrisTian and Megan is beginning To feel lefT out and envious of JuaniTa. AfTer all, Megan Thinks, she's noT ThaT perfecT.

I Do.

Comparing yourself To your friends is never a good idea! You'll end up disliking yourself and losing your friends or being full of pride. Thinking you're beTTer Than your friends.

God made all of us special wiTh differenT TalenTs and abiliTies so ThaT we can work TogeTher! WhaT are Two special TalenTs you have ThaT you can use This week?

Pulse Friends

The Big Idea

Unresolved anger can put an end to even the best of friendships.

Session Aims

In this session you will guide students to:

- Learn that anger is powerful and can bring an end to friendships;
- Feel the desire to resolve anger in their friendships;
- Act by forgiving their friends who make them angry.

The Biggest Verse

"For Saul said to himself, 'I will not raise a hand against him. Let the Philistines do that!'"
1 Samuel 18:17

Other Important Verses

1 Samuel 18:10-17,20-29;
19—20:42;
Proverbs 12:16; 15:1; 29:11;
Matthew 5:23,24,44;
Ephesians 4:26,27,31;
Colossians 3:13; James 1:19

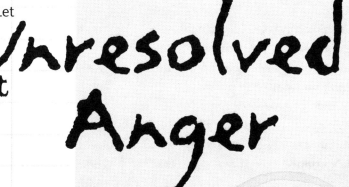

Unresolved Anger

STEP

MOVING IN

This step shows students the powerful effects of anger.

Option 1 Move It

You'll need One adult staff member or volunteer.

Ahead of time, get together with the volunteer and go through the following ad-lib anger scenario.

As students are gathering together, begin the confrontation:

You: **Hey, _____, did you pick up the chocolate bars I asked you to get?**

Volunteer (nonchalantly): **No, sorry, I didn't get around to it.**

You (quite miffed): **You could have let me know! I would have done it myself if I knew you couldn't do it.**

Volunteer: **I didn't think it was that big a deal...**

You (quickly snapping): **I *told* you I needed it for our youth meeting today. I *said* it was part of the lesson! Now I can't do what I had planned!**

Volunteer: **Sorry! I didn't think you'd get so upset!**

You: **Of course I'm upset! I called you ahead of time and made these plans and now they've fallen through. You've ruined everything!**

At this point, the two of you can stop and let the group in on the scheme. Explain: **Today we're going to talk about anger and how it can affect friendships. (Name of volunteer) and I just gave you a taste of how anger can creep into everyday life. It's a powerful emotion, and if we're not careful, it can ruin even the best of friendships.** Read Ephesians 4:26,27. **We learn from this passage that anger itself is not a sin, but it can become a sin if we don't handle it well. So let's learn together how to handle it well.**

Option 2 Chat Room

You'll need Copies of "Rate Your Rage" (p. 88) and pens or pencils.

Greet students and introduce this lesson by explaining: **We'll be talking today about anger and how it affects friendships. First, we're going to rate our own anger levels.** Distribute pens or pencils and "Rate Your Rage" and allow students a couple of minutes to complete the handout. Discuss each situation and encourage students to share why they gave themselves the ratings that they did. Invite them to share their total Rage Rate with the rest of the group.

Transition to the next step by explaining: **Anger is a powerful emotion. It affects how we feel and act toward others. As we're going to see, the Bible has a lot to say about anger.** Read Ephesians 4:26,27. **We learn in this passage that anger itself is not a sin, but it can become a sin if we don't handle it well. So let's learn together how to handle it well.**

Option 3 Fun and Games

You'll need Three ears of corn, paper towels (for cleanup) and a large plastic tarp.

Ahead of time, cook the corn just before the meeting and lay out the plastic tarp.

Greet students and ask for six volunteers who are hungry. Pair them up so you have three teams, then explain: **Today I'm going to give each pair an ear of corn for a snack. One member of each pair will hold the corn while the other one holds his or her hands behind his or her back and eats the corn. In order to win, you must eat at least 90 percent of the corn that is on the cob. Sounds pretty easy, right? Oh, there's one thing I forgot: The one holding the corn can only use his or her feet to hold it. Feel free to remove your shoes and socks if you want, but if you use your hands, your team is out.** Divide the rest of your students into three sections, asking each section to cheer for a different pair of corn-eating contestants.[1]

Once you have a winning pair, congratulate them and have the volunteers return to their seats. Explain: **Corn is one of my favorite things to eat, but I hate it when it gets stuck in my teeth.** Ask the three corn-eating volunteers: **Do any of you have any corn still stuck in your teeth? How does it feel?** Yucky, gross, uncomfortable, aggravating. Continue: **Now let's say you never brushed or flossed your teeth and that corn stayed stuck between your teeth. It would produce bacteria that would release an acid which someday would rot your gums and cause your teeth to fall out. Not a very pleasant thought, is it? Well, today we're going to study something that can also make us pretty rotten. We're going to learn about anger, and the way that it can rot a friendship if we don't do anything about it.**

STEP 2 MOVING UP

This step will show students that anger can kill a friendship.

Option 1 Move It

You'll need Your Bible, copies of "Vehicles of Anger" (p. 89) and pens or pencils.

Begin by explaining: **Just as a car accident can be anything from a scratch to a full-fledged collision, we express our anger in anything from a cutting remark to acts of physical violence.** Ask students to get into groups of three or four and distribute pens or pencils and "Vehicles of Anger." Instruct them to spend a couple of minutes reading it over, circling which kind of car accident they would be, and then sharing what they circled with the rest of the group.

Continue: **In our continuing story about David and King Saul, we find that Saul's feelings of jealousy have turned into fits of rage and violence.** Next, read 1 Samuel 18:10-16. Ask: **In this passage, how would you describe Saul's anger in relation to a "vehicle of anger?" In 1 Samuel 18:29, we learn that "Saul became still more afraid of him, and he remained his enemy the rest of his days." Saul and David used to be friends. How did Saul's anger affect their friendship?** It caused fear and resentment and kept them apart because David had to flee to protect his life.

Transition to the next step by explaining that anger is a human emotion and most of us experience anger at some point in our friendships. That's bad news. The good news is that there *are* ways to resolve it!

Bible Bonus Note

Anger doesn't pay: In 1 Samuel 18:13,14, Saul was so angry with David that he sent him away to battle, just hoping that he would get killed and that would be the end of his rival. But David not only survived, he was a great success. Then Saul tried to trick David into getting killed in a feat he had to perform to marry Michal, Saul's daughter. Once again David was successful and Michal only loved David more (vv. 20-29) and even helped him escape her father (19:11-16). Then Saul tried to get Jonathan to kill David which only resulted in strengthening Jonathan and David's friendship (19:1–20:42). Each time Saul lashed out in anger, he came out the loser, sinking lower and lower. Yet everything David did, God blessed and gave him great success.

Option 2  Chat Room

You'll need Several Bibles, a TV, a VCR and the video *The Prince of Egypt.*

Ahead of time, cue the video approximately 30 minutes from the opening scene to the scene where Moses gets angry at one of the slave masters and kills him.

Show the video clip and explain: **Anger can show itself in many forms. As we just saw in the true story of Moses, Moses reacted to his anger by lashing out and even killing a person. This is similar to the reaction we see in another Bible story about David and King Saul. The outcome is different, but the reaction is similar.**

Invite students to follow along in their Bibles as you read 1 Samuel 18:10-17,29. Discuss the following questions:

It mentions a couple of times in this passage that Saul was afraid of David. What do you think he was afraid of? David's growing popularity and favor with the people; David's skill and talents.

Can you think of times in your friendships when fear turned into anger?

When did Saul's feelings of anger turn into actions of anger?

Can you think of any times when your own anger turned into destructive actions?

Transition to the next step by explaining: **Let's move on to the next step and find out how to resolve feelings of anger before they turn into actions of anger.**

Option 3  Pulse Points

You'll need Your Bible and a bag of ice cubes in a small cooler.

The Big Idea
Anger can lead to destructive actions.

The Big Question
Will we let forgiveness melt away any anger toward others?

1. Anger can hurt.
Give each student a piece of ice and ask them to hold onto their ice while you read 1 Samuel 18:10-17,29 and explain: **Saul's anger toward David went beyond feelings. It moved into actions, violent actions. He was so afraid, jealous and angry at David that he tried to kill him—not just once but many times!**

Invite students to try to hold on tightly to the piece of ice in their hand. See how long they can keep their fists closed before it hurts and they let go.

Explain: **Eventually, the coldness of the ice hurts. That's exactly what happened to Saul's anger towards David. Saul didn't let go of the anger and it finally became painful. The same can happen in our friendships. But there is a way to resolve it.**

2. Anger can destroy.
Ask students to continue to hold their ice cubes as you explain: **Hail is a little thing that can devastate crops, injure animals, pound people, damage aircraft and dent cars. These ice balls come in all sizes, from a tiny pellet to the size of a grapefruit. Hail is formed when a cloud is blown by a violent wind, causing it to rise into the freezing zone in the atmosphere. At that point, ice builds up around the nucleus of a snow pellet. The higher and longer the thunderstorm tosses the particles around, the larger and more destructive the hailstones become, until eventually they are so heavy that they fall to the ground.**

The piece of ice that you're holding in your hand could easily be the size of actual hail. Although it would have started as a tiny pellet of moisture, it would grow in size as it got bounced around.

Hail from a thundercloud and a person's anger have a lot in common. If feelings of anger are not resolved, violent winds of bitterness and hurt feelings can carry the level of anger higher and higher and make it grow even bigger. Pretty soon the feelings of anger get so heavy that they spill out in verbal (or even physical) attacks on others, either directly or behind their backs. If these feelings of anger are not dealt with, they grow into actions of anger that can damage a friendship, just like a hailstorm can damage property and people.

3. Forgiveness can heal.
Ask: **What's happening to the ice cube in your hand the longer you hold it?** It's melting. **Exactly! There are things we can do to melt our anger toward a friend. One of the best things to do is to *forgive*. Friendships are restored when friends forgive each other for the pain caused when they were angry at each other.**

STEP 3

MOVING ON

This step will help students feel motivated to resolve their anger with friends in the right way.

Option 1 Chat Room

You'll need Several boiled or baked potatoes, one for every three to four students.

Ahead of time, plan accordingly, because the potatoes should be hot by the time you reach this step. You can wrap them in towels and brown paper bags to keep them warm for 20-30 minutes. Yes, it's more work, but it makes a good point!

Divide students into groups of four or five and tell them they are going to share about the last time they got mad, which may very well have been earlier that day. It can be anything from "My brother made us late for school this morning because he dumped his cereal bowl" to "My math teacher gave us a ton of homework and it's due tomorrow."

Here's the catch. Each group is going to be handed a very hot potato. The first person who gets it begins sharing but can only talk as long as they are holding the potato. As soon as they pass it to the next person, it becomes his or her turn to share, and so on. The hot potato continues to get passed around the group, and since they can only talk when they're holding the potato, it may take several rounds to finish a story.

During the first round, students will only be able to blurt out one or two words before they have to toss it to the next person. Eventually the potato will cool down and they'll be able to hold it longer and finish their story.

Allow enough time after the potatoes have cooled for the groups to discuss anger, then explain: **Anger is like a hot potato. It's hard to deal with when it's so hot! Once our anger cools down, it's easier to deal with in a gentle and logical manner. Sometimes it's best to let our anger cool before dealing with the issue. Proverbs 29:11 warns us "A fool gives full vent to his anger, but a wise man keeps himself under control," and in Proverbs 12:16 we learn**

that "A fool shows his annoyance at once, but a prudent man overlooks an insult." How does this relate to the hot potato? Once we cool down, we'll be better able to deal with our anger in the right way.

Option 2 Real Life

You'll need Copies of "Reactions to Anger" (p. 90) and pens or pencils.

Ask students to listen carefully as you read the story on the handout.

Explain as you distribute pens or pencils and "Reactions to Anger": **Each of these friends reacted to Scott in a different way. On this handout, try to identify who's who.** The answers are: the Clam is Kalyn; the Outburst is Jamie; the Avenger is Brandon; the Accuser is Curtis; and the Diplomat is Meagan.

After a few minutes, ask students to share their answers. As volunteers share their responses, have each one choose another student to read the scripture that follows his/her answer.

Transition to the next step by asking students to silently choose a description that best fits them. Then explain: **Anger is a part of our human makeup. Though it may not be a sin to become angry, our reactions often become sinful, as Paul reminds us in Ephesians 4:26,27: "In your anger do not sin…do not give the devil a foothold."**

Option 3 Tough Questions

You'll need Several Bibles.

Discuss the following questions and be ready for some honest answers!

1. **When is it wrong to become angry? When is it right to become angry?** It's wrong to become angry for the wrong reasons, like our own selfishness or jealousy. However, if we become justifiably angry because someone has disrespected or hurt us or others, anger is an emotion that follows naturally, and even, get this, an emotion that God created in us. The Bible does teach, though, "In your anger do not sin…do not give the devil a foothold" (Ephesians 4:26,27).

2. **Many psychologists believe that anger, like all emotions, is something that is out of our control, so we should stop trying to control it and express it to release the emotion. How would you respond to this, given what you know about what the Bible says about anger?** In a sense the psychologists are right because anger has a physiological reaction. In other words, our bodies respond with an increased heart rate, dilated pupils, production of adrenaline and increased blood flow to the muscles. And there's nothing we can do about it. God created this response for our protection from danger. However, and this is a *big* HOWEVER, God says we can control our reactions to the emotion of anger, so that in our anger we do not sin (see Ephesians 4:26,27). We can make our anger not sinful if we are quick to forgive others or if we channel it toward making a bad situation better.

3. **What do you think Jesus meant in Matthew 5:44, "But I tell you: Love your enemies and pray for those who persecute you"?** We should not react with anger to those who do wrong to us. Not only should we not get angry, we should go the next step and love them and pray for them.

4. **How should God's forgiveness to us make a difference in how we treat others?** If we remember that God forgives us for our wrongs, we should be quick to forgive others for their wrongs. As Paul writes in Colossians 3:13, "Bear with each other and forgive whatever grievances you may have against one another. Forgive as the Lord forgave you."

5. **What do I do when someone is mad at me, even if I think I haven't really done anything?** Try to figure out if there is anything you've done, no matter how small, that was wrong. There probably is or there might just be a misunderstanding that needs to be cleared up. Just like Jesus says in Matthew 5:23,24, go to the person who is angry with you and ask his or her forgiveness for it. In addition, make sure you let the person know that you'd like to be friends again. Pray that God will help you to be friends again.

STEP 4 — MOVING OUT

This step will encourage students to forgive anyone who makes them angry this week.

Option 1 — Light the Fire

You'll need One adhesive bandage for each student.

Begin by explaining: **Anger can easily creep into any relationship. It's a part of life because it's a part of our human nature, but it does not excuse us to express words that hurt. Instead, we should find ways to cure our anger and mend the relationship.**

Distribute the adhesive bandages to students as you continue: **Stick this bandage in a pocket or somewhere where you'll have immediate access to it during the next week. The next time you get angry with a friend, before you speak or respond in any way, simply take out the bandage, open it and place it on the back of your right hand where you'll see it the rest of the day.**

This will remind you to keep quiet until you calm down so that you don't immediately react in your anger. Not only that, it will be a visual reminder later in the day to go back and deal with the situation. By that time, hopefully your anger will have cooled down, then you'll be able to resolve the situation without such strong feelings of anger.

Close the lesson by praying that God would give students the strength to control their reactions to anger and avoid any damage to their friendships.

Option 2 — Fired Up

You'll need One dime for each student.

Distribute one dime to each student. Now that you've discussed anger, how it can hurt, and how to deal with it, explain that you're going to give everyone a challenge. Invite them to hold the dime and look at it as you give these instructions: **You've heard the phrase, "Count to**

10." Well, here's a way to count to 10, but it will take much longer. The next time you become angry with someone, take out the dime and ask around for change for a dime. You're not allowed to talk to the person who made you angry until you find change for the dime, and here's the clincher: It must be 10 pennies—no nickels allowed.

When you finally get 10 pennies, return to your friend and ask her to hold out her hand. Give her a penny, and as you do, state one reason why you like her and what makes her such a good friend. Do this until you have used up all 10 pennies, giving her 10 reasons. At the end, confess to her that you were angry and why you were angry and tell her you forgive her. It's possible that your friend might end up getting mad at you if you act as if you are better than her, so make sure you continue to affirm her and your friendship the whole time.

This is a challenging exercise, but tell students that you have confidence that they have the maturity to count to 10!

Close the session by praying for strong, mature friendships and that God would help us to forgive so that we can be forgiven.

Option 3  Spread the Fire

You'll need Cotton balls, copies of "Soft Words" (p. 91) and several bottles of glue.

Ahead of time, cut the copied handouts into individual cards.

Distribute the "Soft Words" cards and give each student a cotton ball. Invite them to glue a cotton ball in the middle of the card as you explain: **A cotton ball is soft, clean, and used to help clean wounds. Many of you have friends who are not Christians yet. A lot of them struggle with tempers and unresolved anger in their lives. In Proverbs 15:1, we learn, "A gentle answer turns away wrath, but a harsh word stirs up anger."**

This card will serve as a reminder to you that a kind word might just help cure someone's anger. Continue: **The next time you see a non-Christian friend get angry, or if that person finds out someone else is angry at him, simply go to him and encourage him with a kind greeting, words of support and a promise to pray for him. Who knows what might someday**

result from your cotton-soft, gentle words? You may even have a chance to tell him how to avoid God's anger by asking Jesus to take over his life and be his Savior.

Encourage students to put the card where they will see it each day. Close by praying that students will be instruments of love and kindness in what can sometimes be an angry world.

Note
1. This was an adaptation of an idea suggested by Jim Burns and Mike DeVries, *Fresh Ideas: Bible Study Outlines and Messages* (Gospel Light, 1998), p. 14.

Rate Your Rage

use the following statements to rate how mad you might get in certain situations.

You're grounded all weekend for not taking out the garbage and you had big plans.

A little upset   Very bothered   Angry
1   2   3   4   5   6   7   8   9   10

Your friends go to a movie together and didn't bother to call you.

A little upset   Very bothered   Angry
1   2   3   4   5   6   7   8   9   10

A seam ripped while you were wearing the new pair of jeans you just bought.

A little upset   Very bothered   Angry
1   2   3   4   5   6   7   8   9   10

You're walking down the hall at school and someone purposely trips you.

A little upset   Very bothered   Angry
1   2   3   4   5   6   7   8   9   10

Add your numbered rankings and list your score:

_____ is your Rage Rate.

Vehicles of Anger

How do you deal with anger? Well, let's say you are a car. If you get angry, your anger shows in one of the following ways:

Just a Scratch: You barely notice! It can be rubbed out in no time. (You're not quick to notice when others do wrong.)

Sideswiped: The other person doesn't even see your anger coming and—BAM— you lash out, a total surprise! (You hold it in for too long and don't deal with it right away, then overreact to the slightest thing.)

Fender Bender: A sure hit, but not too strong; a little repair will make it like new. (When you get angry, you resolve it and make things better.)

Rear-end Collision: You impact others from behind. (You tell others instead of the person you're mad at. You're afraid to confront someone who has hurt you.)

Head-on Collision: You cause a heavy, full-on impact with lots of damage. (You tend to blow up and speak without thinking, causing terrible damage to the friendship.)

Reactions to Anger

Jamie, Kalyn, Curtis, Meagan and Brandon were all good friends. They had grown up together and were now in the seventh grade. Jamie's older brother Scott promised to drive all of them to the mountains the upcoming weekend to ski. They've been planning this trip for over a month and can't wait to go.

Two days before the trip, Jamie called all of her friends to tell them that Scott had changed his mind and was spending the weekend with friends from out of town. Jamie's first response to her brother was outrage and harsh words. She yelled at him and blamed him for ruining the whole weekend for her and her friends.

After school the next day, all of her friends came over to her house. Scott was sitting on the living-room couch when they came in. When he said hi to Kalyn, she looked right at him, didn't answer and turned away. Curtis, however, confronted him and said, "That's pretty rude of you to let us down like that. You ruined our whole weekend. Thanks a lot!" Meagan, on the other hand, tried to talk to Scott and ask him why he changed his mind. She really wanted answers.

As they were all leaving that night, Brandon took out his house key and made a small scratch on Scott's car on his way out. No one saw him do it.

Read the descriptions below and match them up with the characters in the story: Jamie, Meagan, Brandon, Kalyn and Curtis.

The Clam: This is the type of person who "clams up" when they're mad. They give the old "cold-shoulder treatment" and are sure to give nonverbal signs that they're upset. When it comes to being angry, they tend to hold it in instead of dealing with it. _____

Ephesians 4:31: "Get rid of all bitterness, rage and anger, brawling and slander, along with every form of malice."

The Outburst: This person doesn't usually think before they speak. Displays of rage and anger are usually their first response to conflict. Their outbursts can be anything from hurtful words to throwing a shoe. _____

James 1:19: "My dear brothers, take note of this: Everyone should be quick to listen, slow to speak and slow to become angry."

The Accuser: This person is one who wants to confront, usually with the intent of accusing. They are "in your face" when it comes to being angry. They don't ignore the situation, but can usually keep their cool. However, they're quick to point the finger. _____

Colossians 3:13: "Bear with each other and forgive whatever grievances you may have against one another. Forgive as the Lord forgave you."

The Diplomat: This person likes to get to the bottom of the problem by talking. They are confrontational in a diplomatic sort of way and want to make sure they have all the facts before coming to a judgment. _____

Proverbs 15:1: "A gentle answer turns away wrath, but a harsh word stirs up anger."

The Avenger: This person can be dangerous when anger sets in. They tend to express their anger by acts of destruction and sometimes violence. Unlike the "Outburst," their actions are thought out with revenge and retaliation in mind. Most times they later regret their actions, but by then it's too late; the damage has been done. _____

Ephesians 4:26,27: "In your anger do not sin. Do not let the sun go down while you are still angry, and do not give the devil a foothold."

Soft Words

"A gentle answer turns away wrath, but a harsh word stirs up anger."
Proverbs 15:1

"A gentle answer turns away wrath, but a harsh word stirs up anger."
Proverbs 15:1

"A GENTLE ANSWER TURNS AWAY WRATH, BUT A HARSH WORD STIRS UP ANGER." PROVERBS 15:1

"A gentle answer turns away wrath, but a harsh word stirs up anger."
Proverbs 15:1

"A genTle answer Turns away wraTh, buT a harsh word sTirs up anger."
Proverbs 1 5:1

"A gentle answer turns away wrath, but a harsh word stirs up anger."
Proverbs 15:1

"A gentle answer turns away wrath, but a harsh word stirs up anger."
Proverbs 15:1

"A gentle answer turns away wrath, but a harsh word stirs up anger."
Proverbs 15:1

Devotions in Motion

WEEK SIX: UNRESOLVED ANGER

DAY 1

Fast Facts

Hey? Don't blink until you've read Matthew 5:21,22.

God Says

In Eli's family, there's a fight almost every day. Everyone yells and curses and tells each other to shut up. So when Eli fights with his friends, he fights the same way, yelling and screaming and calling them foul names. "It's no big deal," he tells his friend Pat when Pat tells him that's a bad way to argue. "That's how I've fought all my life, and besides, it's not like I mean it when I call you names. Don't be so sensitive."

I Do

Lots of people do things they regret later when they're upset with someone, especially when that someone is a friend or family member. When you fight with your friends (and everybody eventually does) are you as calm and honest as you can be? Or do you try and hurt your friend the way he or she hurt you, calling him or her names and being cruel?

Ask God to help you love your friends, even when they do something that hurts you.

FOLD HERE ---

DAY 4

Quick Questions

Dive into Proverbs 17:17 and see what a friend is.

God Says

When is it easiest to love your friends:

- [ ] When they bring you a plate of warm chocolate-chip cookies?
- [ ] When they help you clean your room?
- [ ] When they tell you they love being your friend?

When is it hardest to love your friends:

- [ ] When they ignore you?
- [ ] When they give one of your secrets away?
- [ ] When you get in a big fight?

When do your friends need your love the most:

- [ ] When their parents are fighting?
- [ ] When they're feeling alone?
- [ ] When they think no one else loves them?

I Do

Loving someone all the time is a pretty tall order, especially if they've hurt you or pushed you away. God is the only one who can give us what we need to give love like that.

Ask God to help you show your friends that you care about them today.

Quick Questions

Race to James 1:19-21 and see what God desires for you.

God Says

What would you feel and do if your best friend said something like this to you?

- ☐ "I don't even know why I'm friends with you. You're so dumb sometimes!"
- ☐ "Can't you see I'm trying to read? Quit bugging me already!"
- ☐ "You don't know anything about it, so why don't you just shut up?"

I Do

Ouch! Some of those things would be really hard to take! If this person really is your friend, however, you need to remember that we're all imperfect. They may be angry at someone else but are taking it out on you. Walk away when they're like that or just ignore them.

Think of what you do when you're angry. Do you fly off the handle and say hurtful things? Do you need to apologize to anyone today for the things you've said when you were mad?

FOLD HERE --

Fast Facts

Get into Ephesians 4:25-27 and see what to do before sunset every day!

God Says

Pam slammed the phone down before Erin could say any more. She was so ticked! How could Erin have been such a jerk—telling Lane that Pam liked him! The next day at school Pam refused to talk to her, and when Erin tried to apologize, Pam turned around and walked away. Pam wouldn't pick up the phone when she called all that weekend and pretty soon Erin stopped trying to call. At school, they wouldn't even look at each other. A few months later, it was summer and Pam missed Erin and Erin missed Pam, but it was too late. It seemed their relationship might be too damaged to repair.

I Do

Don't let that happen to you! Listen to your friends when they want to apologize, even if you still feel hurt. Accept their apologies and take the opportunity to talk things out. And when you hurt one of your friends, do everything you can to make it right.

HOW TO SAY YOU'RE SORRY TO GOD AND YOUR FRIENDS

Words by themselves are cheap! The only way to truly say you're sorry is to change the *actions* that offended God or another person. That's what the Bible refers to as repentance (see Acts 26:20).

It's only through the process of repentance that we can seek forgiveness and it's only through God's forgiveness that we are cleansed of our sins. The following letter was written to a man on death row by the father of the man he killed. When you're done reading the letter, try to figure out which famous father might have written it.

On the Move

You are probably surprised that I, of all people, am writing a letter to you. But as the father of the man you helped to murder, I have something very important to say to you: I forgive you.

With all my heart, I forgive you. I realize it may be hard for you to believe, but I really do. At your trial, when you showed your sorrow for your part in the events that cost my son his life and asked for my forgiveness, I immediately granted you that forgiving love. I can only hope you believe me and will accept my forgiveness.

But that is not all I have to say to you. I want to make you an offer. I want you to become my adopted child. You see, my son who died was my only child, and now I want to share my life with you and leave my riches to you. This may not make sense to you or anyone else, but I believe you are worth the offer. I have arranged matters so that if you will receive my offer of forgiveness, not only will you be pardoned for your crime, but your death sentence will be dismissed and you will be set free from your imprisonment. You will become my adopted child and heir to all my riches.

Have you guessed who this famous father is? Turn the paper upside down to read the answer.

Maybe you guessed who the father was or maybe you didn't, but the truth is that once you repent to God for whatever you've done, He wipes the sin away--it's gone. And so is that guilty feeling you have when you know you've done something wrong (see 1 John 1:9). That's why you should admit your misdeeds to God--or to anyone else, for that matter.

But what about figuring out *how* to say you're sorry? Here are some big truths to keep in mind:

3 Big STeps

The word Jesus uses for saying you're sorry is "repenT," which means To "Turn from sin." When you do someThing wrong, you Take Three big sTeps in repenTing:

1. You admiT your misTake, Taking ownership over iT;
2. You Turn from iT and change your acTions, so ThaT you don'T repeaT iT;
3. You seek resTiTuTion To correcT The wrongdoing.

For example: LeT's say you've borrowed your besT friend's sweaTshirT and carelessly spilled grape juice all over iT and couldn'T geT The sTain ouT. FirsT, Tell your friend abouT your misTake, apologizing for your carelessness (Taking ownership). Second, promise To be more careful in The fuTure (changing your acTions) and Third, ask your friend how you can replace his/her sweaTshirT—buy him/her a new one or maybe giving him/her one of your favoriTes (resTiTuTion). GeT iT?

2 Big Types

There are Two big Types of Things ThaT you mighT need To be sorry for. Here are some examples and appropriaTe acTions To Take To repenT:

1. You've done someThing wrong.
   - You gossiped abouT a new kid in school. Remove yourself from all gossip and inTroduce yourself To The kid, remembering ThaT you are an example of Jesus' love.
   - You were swearing during a fooTball game aT P. E. Ask God for forgiveness and make sure To use your words To honor Him in The fuTure!

2. You haven'T done someThing righT.
   - A new sTudenT aT your school dropped his Tray during lunch Today. You didn'T laugh aT him like everyone else, buT you also didn'T help him ouT because The oTher sTudenTs mighT laugh aT you, Too. The nexT Time you see someone who needs a helping hand, be The firsT in line To help!
   - You didn'T pray before you headed off To school Tomorrow, seT your alarm five minuTes earlier and spend ThaT exTra Time wiTh God.

1 Big AcTion

Every day you will do someThing wrong or you won'T do someThing righT, which can hurT your friends and Take you furTher away from God. The more you use The sTeps of repenTance, The more iT becomes a habiT. The more repenTance becomes a habiT, The easier iT is.

ThroughouT hisTory, God has done big Things, like resolving argumenTs, ending addicTions and mending broken hearTs—all because someone recognized Their own wrongdoing and repenTed. Anyone—even you—who learns To say "I'm sorry" To God, family and friends can be parT of a new revival in a family, church, school or ciTy. WhaT an awesome opporTuniTy you have!

THE FATHER IS GOD.